IMAGES
of America

UPPER TOWNSHIP
AND ITS TEN VILLAGES

Robert F. Holden

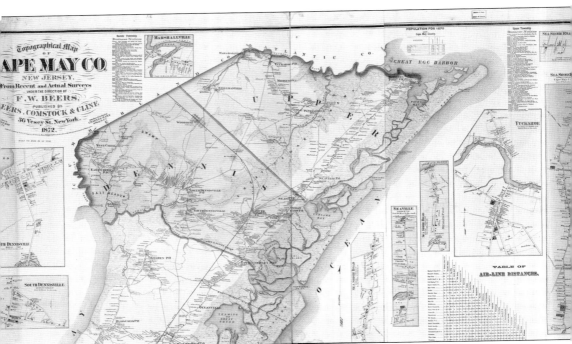

This 1872 topographical map of Cape May County, New Jersey, by F.W. Beers shows Upper Township, located at the top. Note the many houses, churches, and other structures along what was once known as Seashore Road. Prior to 1827, Dennis Township and Upper Township made up what was called Upper Precinct, but here, there is a clear border between the two. Due to having received its own post office as part of Dennis Township, Ocean View, the home of Upper Township's founder, John Townsend, is no longer a part of Upper Township. (Courtesy of Library of Congress, Geography and Map Division.)

ON THE COVER: This c. 1906–1910 photograph shows the Tuckahoe train station, built in 1894. A short time later, Tuckahoe was a rail hub for the township; by 1910, speculators and developers were selling lots nearby for building homes. Standing in front of the station with his horse-drawn wagon and dog is Giro Migliaccio, the grandfather of Upper Township resident Joan Wood. Migliaccio planted the surrounding gardens and took people and baggage from the station to the Tuckahoe Hotel and other local destinations. (Courtesy of the Historical Preservation Society of Upper Township.)

IMAGES
of America

UPPER TOWNSHIP
AND ITS TEN VILLAGES

Robert F. Holden with the
Historical Preservation Society of Upper Township

ARCADIA
PUBLISHING

Published by Arcadia Publishing
Charleston, South Carolina

Printed in the United States of America

Library of Congress Control Number: 2019946580

For all general information, please contact Arcadia Publishing:
Telephone 843-853-2070
Fax 843-853-0044
E-mail sales@arcadiapublishing.com
For customer service and orders:
Toll-Free 1-888-313-2665

Visit us on the Internet at www.arcadiapublishing.com

I dedicate this book to my two young granddaughters, Amelia and Harper—their love of books inspired me to write this, which I hope they one day read and enjoy as children raised in wonderful Upper Township.

CONTENTS

ACKNOWLEDGMENTS

This book owes its heart to the writers who preceded me in the 1989 book *A History of Upper Township and Its Villages*, published by the Historical Preservation Society of Upper Township (HPSUT), especially Florence Speck, Mary Jane Corson, Jane Corson, Edgar Y. Corson, Anthony Butler, Clare Campbell, Jean Albrecht, Joyce Van Vorst, William Tullner, Alwina D. Bailey, Margaret Folger, Katherine Carmona, and Harry P. Folger III. The book included a wide variety of authors, many not historians but just folks who loved Upper Township. Without it, I could not have had an adequate jumping-off point. I am grateful for their work.

In gathering photographs of the township I relied heavily on just a few contributors, although I met with dozens of wonderful people. I am most grateful to Barbara Horan; Sharon Lynne Dress; Mike Houdart; Grace and Tom Garrity, who met with me to go over scanned photographs and provided details I would have never known; and Sonia Forry, the historical society's previous historian, who proofread my introductions.

I am also grateful to the Board of Trustees of the Historical Preservation Society of Upper Township, which was fully behind this project when first proposed.

I must also thank the following contributors of so many great photographs of our township, in no particular order: Ray Rebmann (Dennisville History Society), Paul Loveland III (Loveland Funeral Home), Corville Griner, Barbara Horan, Sharon Lynne Dress, Harriett Reardon Bailey (Endicott Reardon Museum), Leonard R. Carlson, Carol Collins, Theodore Kayiales (Tuckahoe Diner, formerly Robinette's), Grace and Tom Garrity, Merry and Joe May, Stoddard and Marge Bixby, Edward Bixby Jr., Carol Baker at Strathmere.net, Nick Karayiannias (Dino's Diner), Colleen Argoe-Super, Curtis Corson Jr., Louise Letsinger, Karen Behr, Jean Campbell, and Harry P. Folger III.

A special thank-you to Grace and Tom Garrity for generously providing funding to help make this book possible!

Thanks also to the folks at Arcadia Publishing, particularly Angel Hisnanick, who guided me and helped beyond measure.

Finally, thanks and love go to my wife, Janice, who unflinchingly supported my efforts to create this book and who tolerated my crowded study and frequent absences whether due to searching for photographs and meeting with people throughout the township or typing and scanning. Her support and belief in me still amaze me after 42 years of marriage.

INTRODUCTION

The first map of Cape May County based on a survey appears to have been made by Lewis Morris in 1706, and the first road giving land connections from north to south was laid out by William Goldin and Shamgar Hand and completed in 1707. The road extended from Beesley's Point to Cold Spring and was known as Seashore Road, present-day Route 9.

The county was first organized in 1692, and its limits were definitely determined in 1710. It remained undivided until 1723, when it was split into three precincts, Lower, Middle, and Upper. In 1827, Upper Precinct, the largest of the three, was divided into Dennis and Upper, and the precincts then became townships.

The earliest inhabitants of this region were Native Americans who belonged to the Lenni Lenape tribe, also known as the Delaware tribe of the Algonquians. These people always adjusted to nature rather than the other way around and were kind, trustful, and peaceable; however, they soon found their hunting grounds, streams, and liberties curtailed by the laws created by white men. However, it must be noted that in New Jersey, white settlers never took land from Indians without purchasing it, and this was especially true when land was purchased by Quakers, Swedes, or the Dutch. There is no way of accurately estimating the number of Indians who lived here, but it is known that interior tribes migrated each spring and summer to the shore, while some lived here all year long. The chief occupations of the Indians of Upper Township were hunting, fishing (fin and shell), and farming, and their primary place of habitation was along the small streams, rivers, and bays.

The Indians of the Beesley's Point area had a campground on the Townsend Stites division of Isaiah Stites's property purchased in 1740. Thomas Stites, son of Townsend and grandson of John Stites and great-grandson of Isaiah, once collected and sold a bushel of various arrowheads. These and other stone artifacts, like tomahawks, spears, knives, and axes, along with shell piles, have been found in Beesley's Point for many years. In fact, on the Stites farm in Beesley's Point there was one field that could never be planted because of the vast amount of lime that leached from the clam and oyster shells. Crops would grow to only half size and then die because of the alkalinity caused by the excessive amounts of shells. South on Shore Road to Palermo, a great many artifacts have been found on local farms. The Curtis Corson family has one of the finest collections of Indian artifacts in South Jersey.

White immigrants inhabited the area by 1691, and Upper Precinct was formed in 1723. Originally, Upper Precinct included Dennis Creek to the Atlantic Ocean, Dennis Township, Sea Isle City, Strathmere, and Peck's Beach (now Ocean City). The northern boundary extended beyond Great Egg Harbor Bay. The western boundary was indefinite until 1878, when the boundaries were finally settled. The township had few villages before the Revolution. They were Goldin's (or Stite's) Point, Littleworth, and Williamsburg. Tuckahoe, one of the largest villages in the township, is the only Indian name remaining.

One of our earliest permanent pioneers was John Townsend, a staunch Quaker who arrived between 1680 and 1685 from Long Island. Quakers had been banished from the New York colony for harboring dissidents, and Townsend was one of them. He sailed down the Jersey coast looking for a suitable place to build a home. After stopping at Leed's Point and then eventually what would be known as Somers Point, he managed to swim his cattle across the Great Egg Harbor Bay and continued to drive them over an old Indian trail (what is now Shore Road/Route 9) to a small run with enough power to operate a mill. By a body of water now known as Magnolia Lake, he decided to build a house and a mill. Christopher Leaming of Town Bank and Joseph Ludlam of Dennis Creek, as well as some local Indians, helped him to dam up the run and build the house and mill. His wife, Phoebe, who died in 1704, was the first white woman buried in Upper Precinct. His son, Richard, was the first white child born here.

Other early families before 1700 were the Corsons, Van Gilders, Ludlams, Leamings, Godfreys, Gandys, and Stiteses. They all came from Long Island for the purpose of whaling. Primary products from whaling were oil for lamps and whale bones for women's garments. Whaling also created the need for coopers, boatbuilders, sailors, lumbermen, and farmers. Additional industries were salt making (by evaporation), shingle mining, lumbering for cedar, and glassmaking. The ships built in Dennis Creek, the Tuckahoe River, and Petersburg carried lumber and all kinds of other commodities to Philadelphia, New York, and other domestic and international ports.

The dominant religion in those early days was Quakerism. While religious freedom was not always the primary motivation for coming here, it was a very important part of the lives of the Corsons, Garretsons, Townsends, Baners, Willets, and others who followed them. As early as 1702, the Quakers, who called themselves Friends, of Upper Precinct first worshipped with the Friends of Egg Harbor Meeting (Somers Point). They held alternative monthly meetings for business in the homes of members. Neither side built a meetinghouse until 1727, when the Beesley's Point side of the bay built a pine and cedar meetinghouse with a cedar shingle roof. This meetinghouse remains standing today, although it is now located in Seaville on South Shore Road. There is no evidence or record in old Friends' meeting minutes as to how it was moved to Seaville from Beesley's Point. For over 100 years, the Quakers were the only denomination to have a meetinghouse, but gradually the Anglicans, Baptists, Presbyterians, and Methodists established their own houses of worship and flourished in Upper Township. The area has long been a place of religious tolerance and peaceful coexistence.

The Township Act of 1798 incorporated the original 103 townships of New Jersey, and Upper was one of those originals. The new law granted the town meeting broad powers, including the ability to tax the people in order to carry out township responsibilities. The town meeting in each township was authorized to elect officials for one year, including a township clerk, tax assessors, tax collectors, three or more "judicious freeholders of good character" to hear tax appeals, overseers of the highways, pound keepers, and one reputable freeholder to serve as a judge of elections.

In 1899, a revision of the act was passed, changing the way the townships were governed. The town meeting was abolished, and all sanctioned municipal legislatures were concentrated in the hands of a stronger township committee. The committee was developed as a policy-making body that was authorized to pass ordinances and make appointments. It was to consist of three members, but later, this was expanded to allow five elected members with staggered three-year terms.

The township today is made up of 10 villages, each of which will be profiled in this book.

One

BEESLEY'S POINT

Beesley's Point, the northernmost village of Upper Township, lies across Great Egg Bay from Somers Point, New Jersey.

Much went on here before Thomas Beesley lived in the area from 1816 until his death in 1849. Quaker settlers first formed a meeting here in 1702 under the supervision of the Salem Quarterly Meeting. Some came by boat from Somers Point (from the Great Egg Harbor Monthly Meeting) for scheduled meetings in Friends' homes. A meetinghouse was constructed somewhere in Beesley's Point in 1727, and continued until it was later moved to Seaville in about 1764.

The first hotel at the point, at that time Goldin's Point, was built and operated by Nicholas Stillwell, son of John, in 1748 on a large piece of plantation land purchased from Joseph Goldin, the grandson of original settler William Goldin. Joseph Goldin owned much of the land in what is now Beesley's Point. Part of it was known as Foxborough Hill in 1736. A tavern license for the Stillwell Inn was issued in 1750.

Isaiah Stites bought the remaining piece of the plantation land from Joseph Goldin around 1736, and opened a tavern across Seashore Road. This land was sold to Stites as part of the court settlement punishing Joseph Goldin for the murder of an Indian.

Nicholas Stillwell died in 1772 and his building was passed down to his son Capt. Nicholas Stillwell, who later sold it to Thomas Borden, who sold it in 1803 to Thomas Beesley. This property was the site of the legendary Revolutionary War incident of the Stillwell sisters repelling a British invasion force. In 1777, Rebecca Stillwell noticed a British gunboat in the bay and shouted a warning that the redcoats were coming. Indeed they were. The British forces had been notified by a local Tory of the ammunition and supplies stored there by local privateers. Rebecca and her sister Sarah loaded and fired a cannon at the British soldiers coming in to land, causing them to return to their ship and sail away. The Stillwell sisters are much celebrated today as Upper Township heroes of the Revolution.

Not much is known today about the tavern, but it is known that Stillwell operated a ferry between the two towns, which started in 1693. The original hotel on the site of what became Beesley's Point passed through several owners: first the Stillwells, then the Bordens, followed by the McCormacks, then the Beesleys, and then to Capt. John Chattin in 1849. In fact, for a very long time the hotel was known as the Chattin House.

In 1848–1849, Richard Stites, descendant of Isaiah Stites, built an even larger hotel opposite the Chattin House on Seashore Road at Stites Point, and the old Chattin House hotel became a private residence for a few decades. The Chattin House was sold in the 1890s to the Beesley's Point Fishing Club, with a membership of prominent Philadelphia and local businessmen and politicians. It was a members-only club. It was dissolved in 1906, and the title to the building was held by member Henry Clay's wife, Savilla. The Clays decided to make it their permanent home in 1915. In the meantime, the Clays had purchased the Beesley's Point Hotel. Upon their deaths, their daughter Mabel became the owner of the home in 1923. When she died, probably in the 1950s, the Chattin House building was sold by her heirs to what became known as the Bay Front Training School, an institution for mentally challenged students eventually known in the 1960s–1970s as Kelly's Home & School for Retarded Students. After it closed in the late 1970s, it was operated as the Beesley's Point Sea-Doo Co. The building was finally demolished on June 5, 2017.

The Stites House on the opposite side of Seashore Road had become quite prosperous, especially since the fishing club across the road had closed, catering to hunting and fishing parties. Stites built two additions over the years. The Beesley's Point Hotel became well known in the area and was sold to the Chattin House owner, Mabel Clay. This newer, larger Beesley's Point Hotel was a center for social affairs in the township. Since Mabel Clay was a prominent and influential woman (she was the Republican state committeewoman), over the years, she organized numerous events at the hotel. One of the last social affairs held in the hotel was the homecoming arranged by local Red Cross branches for returning World War I soldiers in 1919.

The area near Beesley's Point Hotel, where the Tuckahoe Inn is located today, became a popular picnic and bathing place in summer. Fishing and sailing parties were daily diversions, and many groups from around the area made their way to Beesley's Point.

In the late 19th century, all freight for the area was sent through Atlantic County to Somers Point, then transported by boat to Beesley's Point in Cape May County. All of the merchandise sold at Ashmead's General Store in Beesley's Point was brought over by boat from Somers Point.

Until 1897, the only way to reach the point was by a long stagecoach ride, by horse and wagon from points farther south in Cape May County, or by sailboat from Somers Point. When the first railroad was built into Ocean City, it passed through Palermo four miles south of the point. Guests arrived by train to Palermo Station and then were taken by horse and wagon to Beesley's Point. In 1928, a toll bridge was built over the bay connecting Shore Road to Route 9 in Somers Point. The bridge consisted of 120 spans and an 80-foot double leaf bascule span (draw bridge) that opened for maritime traffic. The bridge was immensely popular for its convenient access to and from Cape May County, and for its low cost (the toll never rose above 50¢.) This stimulated a land boom in the township.

The Beesley's Point Hotel closed during the Depression but reopened sometime prior to 1949, advertising a bar, cocktail lounge, and dining room with accommodations for banquets and weddings. In 1962, a fire destroyed the building and the Charles Harp family of Ocean City purchased what was left of it and built a brand-new structure in 1963, today known as the Tuckahoe Inn, named for the first inhabitants of the area, the Tuckahoe Indians. Charlie Harp's son Peter worked in the business for over 33 years and finally sold the landmark business to the Merriman family, which continues the tradition of fine dining today. The Beesley's Point Bridge that ran right beside the inn closed in 2004 and was eventually demolished.

Beesley's Point was always populated; over the years, several schools were located there. The Beesley's Point School was built in 1889 across the street from the township's third school, built in 1816, and was in use until 1954. It closed when the township consolidated its schools. Today it is a private home. The township has also built two elementary schools nearby in Marmora.

Today, Beesley's Point is a community with a few businesses, the major one being the B.L. England power plant built at the tip of the point in 1963. The plant, originally coal fired, supplied electricity for the surrounding area and provided a wonderful tax base for the township, providing the bulk of the general-purpose tax, lowering property taxes for all residents. The power plant has been permanently closed. What will be built on the property is yet to be determined.

Beesley's Point is a quiet section of the township containing some of its richest history.

The Ashmead Country Store on the corner of Seashore and Beesley's Roads was the only store in Beesley's Point at the time of this 1900 photograph. Goods for the store were brought by ferry over from Somers Point. In the 1920s, the building was moved and attached to Stratton's store. (Courtesy of HPSUT.)

In this 1900 photograph of the Beesley's Point School on Seashore Road is the class and teacher Sally van Gilder. This building replaced the original schoolhouse, which was moved to Ocean City to be used as a barn. It was built on land deeded to the trustees in 1818 for $40. It was a subscription school until 1853. (Courtesy of HPSUT.)

Beesley's Point Hotel, Beesley's Point, N. J.

This is a fascinating c. 1900 photograph of the original Beesley's Point Hotel, built on the site of the Stites Tavern. This building burned to the ground (year unknown), and the newer, larger Beesley's Point Hotel was built in its place. (Courtesy of HPSUT.)

Joseph Goldin's house was part of a very large plantation. Goldin sold off part of his land to Nicholas Stillwell in 1736, and then sold the remaining part to Isaiah Stites in 1740 after a court case resulted in a fine for Goldin's murder of a Native American, which was ruled unintentional. Goldin then moved to a house on Willet's Point. (Courtesy of HPSUT.)

ORIGINAL PIER AT BEESLEY'S POINT

PHOTO BY H.F.WITMER 1890

Long before the Beesley's Point Bridge was built, all traffic and goods from the north to Beesley's Point came by boat or ferry. This rare photograph shows the original Beesley's Point Pier. The photograph, taken in 1890 by H.F. Witmer, was likely taken from the site of the Beesley's Point Hotel. (Courtesy of HPSUT.)

This is a photograph of the Stillwell House, which became the Chattin House hotel, the Clays' home, the Beesley's Point Fishing Club, and eventually, the Bayfront Training School. The building's final occupant was a Sea-Doo rental company, which was popular with tourists. (Courtesy of HPSUT.)

Here is a crisp photograph of the original Upper Township Municipal Building. It was moved first to Beesley's Point and used as a store. Later, Cold Spring Village, a collection of old buildings gathered from throughout the county, in Lower Township, Cape May County, purchased it, and it still stands there today. (Courtesy of HPSUT.)

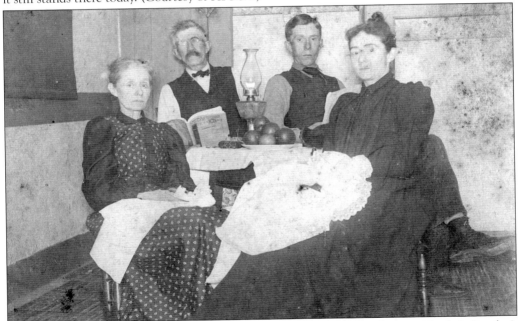

This charming early-20th-century photograph is of Stites family members inside their Beesley's Point home. Sitting around the table are, from left to right, Elizabeth Stites (mother), Thomas B. Stites (father), Morris Beesley Stites, and Hattie Stites. The men are reading, and the women are working on their sewing. Note the lit oil lamp and plate of apples. (Courtesy of Barbara Horan.)

This c. 1910 photograph shows students of Beesley's Point School. The teacher is Jake Townsend. This building is now a private home. (Courtesy of HPSUT.)

The Eli and Mary Burnell House (also known as the Henry Young House of the Young plantation of Beesley's Point) was built between 1815 and 1825 in the Federal style. The Young plantation was one of the largest in the area. The house was built on Seashore Road (Route 9) and still stands today. (Courtesy of HPSUT.)

The Reuben Corson house in Beesley's Point still stands today. It is reported to have had the first functioning telephone in Upper Township. (Courtesy of HPSUT.)

Beesley's Point Hotel, Beesley's Point, N. J.

This version of the Beesley's Point Hotel was built in 1849 by Richard Stites as an addition to the original tavern (1736). Operated as a hotel through 1909, the hotel remained open through World War II but closed briefly afterward. It reopened in the late 1940s and burned down in 1962. The Harp family bought the property and later built the Tuckahoe Inn on the site. (Courtesy of HPSUT.)

This wonderful photograph was taken on the steps of the Beesley's Point Hotel in 1919, at the end of World War I. Young veterans are standing behind older veterans of the Civil War. Their officers are in front of them. The men seated in the very front are Union Army veterans of the Civil War, who were members of the Grand Army of the Republic. Among them is Horace Townsend (second from right), the great-great-grandfather of Sharon Lynne Dress of Upper Township. (Courtesy of HPSUT.)

Nursing played a large part during World War I, both at home and overseas. This photograph, taken during or just after the Great War, shows Red Cross nurses from Beesley's Point, Palermo, and Petersburg on the front steps of the Beesley's Point Hotel. It is believed that their service to the war effort was being acknowledged. (Courtesy of Curtis Corson Jr.)

This interesting photograph shows construction on the Somers Point side of the Beesley's Point Bridge. Since the bridge was completed in 1928, the picture was likely taken in about 1926–1927. (Courtesy of Grace and Tom Garrity.)

The grand opening of the new Beesley's Point Bridge took place in June 1928. The bridge was planned and built by a group of businessmen who wanted residents to travel more easily between Atlantic and Cape May Counties. The cost to cross one way remained 25¢ into the 1980s. It became structurally unsound and was removed in 2016. (Courtesy of HPSUT.)

This is a modern postcard of the Tuckahoe Inn, built by the Harp family on the original site of the 1736 Stites Tavern, Stites Hotel, and Beesley's Point Hotel, which burned down in 1962. The inn pays tribute to the original Stites Tavern with the date "1736" on its chimney. Although a popular restaurant, lodging is no longer available at the inn. (Courtesy of HPSUT.)

The Garden State Parkway stretched from Cape May (Exit 0) north to Montvale (Exit 172) and opened in September 1954. This postcard shows what the toll plazas looked like when new. The parkway was a faster route to the seashore, but it created some economic hardship for businesses that depended on tourist traffic through small villages. (Courtesy of Linda Leonard, HPSUT.)

The B.L. England generating station was built in 1963 at Beesley's Point. The power plant was a tax bonus for Upper Township residents because of the local-purpose tax, which reduced the overall tax rate for every property owner in the township. The plant went from multiple stacks to a single higher stack with scrubbers to better clean the air. It closed in May 2019 due to controversy over proposed fuels to be used to power it and problematic technologies. (Courtesy of Grace and Tom Garrity.)

Here is yet another interesting picture taken on the steps of the Beesley's Point Hotel in about 1920. (It could have been taken the same day as the veterans' photograph on page 17.) This one shows local businessmen and politicians. Notable names include Henry Clay, Lewis Cresse, Dr. Randolph Marshall Jr., Hope W. Gandy, Robert S. Miller, E.V. Corson, Harry Snyder, Clayton Haines Brick, Samuel G. Corson, Frank S. Ashmead Sr., Frank Creama, E.L. Rice, and Walter and Harvey Taylor. (Courtesy of HPSUT.)

Two

MARMORA

The old village of Marmora, now the "downtown" of Upper Township, due south of Beesley's Point on Shore Road, had few settlers before it was called Marmora. The village had a section between Beesley's Point and Marmora called Miramar as late as 1926, according to an early survey map of Ocean City. It was not a separate village, but a northern neighborhood section of Marmora whose streets are still there. Some of the original area of Marmora was part of Thomas Beesley's land and the area was nicknamed "Beesleys."

The Leni-Lenape, part of the Algonquin Indian group, were the first to live in the area, coming here to bathe, fish, and gather clams. There was once a large shell pile on the Willets plantation at Miller Creek; many native American artifacts were found there. The appearance of white men discouraged the natives' return.

The people of Marmora earned their living as farmers, going off to sea, or becoming soldiers, some fighting in our early wars. The farms, known as plantations, were quite large. Two of the largest were the Willets plantation owned by Dr. Jacob Willets and the Stephen Young plantation.

Slavery existed in New Jersey from the 17th century until 1865 (New Jersey was the last state to officially end slavery), and with large plantations, labor was in high demand, so some farmers surely saw the need for slaves to work their land. One slave in particular named Sal was permitted to run the Willets plantation due to her age and skills. This was extremely unusual for the time. Sal was even buried on the plantation in the family plot.

Most large farms were purchased from the West Jersey Society, a joint stock company composed of 48 citizen investors, mostly living in London. The names of Queen Anne and King George of England appear in the very early deeds.

Trinity Methodist Church was built in 1869 at the corner of Seashore Road and what would later be called Roosevelt Boulevard. It later became the Seventh Day Adventist Church when Trinity built a new church north of the corner.

As the decades went by, farms remained much the same, but at the turn of the 20th century, things began to change. Development began to stretch its tentacles throughout this once rural, placid landscape. The Willets plantation was developed into housing tracts in 1926 and was called West Ocean City. This is also where the neighborhood of Miramar was located. All of this is now the Village of Marmora. Early settlers of Marmora included the Godfreys, Garretsons, Corsons, and Youngs. Some of them lived along the Woods Road, also known as the Backroad (later Old Stagecoach Road), which ran parallel to Shore Road.

The children of Marmora attended the "Farmers School" (School No. 1) in Beesley's Point. It was built in 1814, but was replaced by School No. 2 in 1889. Parents had to pay tuition. The School No. 2 building still stands as a private home.

Quakers, Baptists, and later Methodists were numerous in Marmora by the late 1700s. Methodism dates to 1736, when John and Charles Wesley began their religious movement. Like Quakers, early Methodists met in members' homes until they could save enough money to build a church.

The area grew quite slowly until after the Revolutionary War.

Legend has it that the village got its name when the first post office was opened on June 21, 1890. The post office was then located on the northwest side of Shore Road in the general store owned by Postmaster Henry Corson, as most were in those days. A local sea captain in the area had apparently once sailed to the Sea of Marmara, located west of Constantinople, and locals who knew him liked the name. However, the village was not named Marmara, but Marmora. There is little to corroborate this story. The post office has had surprisingly few postmasters since its opening. Early postmasters were Joseph H. Corson, 1890 and again in 1898; Stephen Young, 1894; Edgar A Stratton, 1907; Wilma Clayton, 1941; Melvin Pashley, 1947; and Ed Getty, 1949 (he bought the Stratton store and gas station during this time).

Joe Henry Corson died and his business was purchased by Edgar Stratton, who bought the store where the post office was located. The building was enlarged by the move of the Ashmead general store building from Beesley's Point before it was purchased by Stratton; probably by Young. The Stratton store was eventually moved back from Route 9 in the 1930s due to a widening project and the post office moved across the street to a separate building. Eventually, the store was purchased by the Claytons, then Ed Getty, the postmaster in 1949, and then by Cody Letsinger and his wife. Known simply as Cody's, it was a popular market selling sandwiches, milk, necessities, and even greeting cards. It even brought folks over from Ocean City for its great sandwiches. Today, the site is occupied by a large chain convenience store and gas station.

The new post office was built across the street on the eastern side of Shore Road, where a jewelry store and dry cleaner shop are located today. As development increased and brought more traffic, it became more problematic to get into and out of the post office parking area. Just south of Stratton's store and Esso gas station was the Collins ice cream store, with a photography studio in the basement, and the Amoco gas station, which opened in the 1930s and was in continuous operation through the late 1950s selling snacks, candy, cigarettes, ice cream, and gasoline to tourists on their way to Ocean City. It was located where Kirk's Pizza is today. The advent of the Garden State Parkway diminished commerce for some businesses in Marmora because travelers now exited the parkway directly for Ocean City, bypassing Marmora.

After World War II, things began to change in the area because of the growth of the seashore resorts, particularly Ocean City directly across the causeway. Many new jobs were created.

Today, Marmora is the business hub of the township along with parts of Seaville and Tuckahoe. The Wayside Village Shops, created in 1974, were once part of a very large farm owned by R. Fendall Smith. The original farmhouse was later moved to Old Stagecoach Road and the farm was sold to developers who created the shopping center. Remnants of this once large farm are nearly all gone, but the current ice cream stand was once the water pump for the farm, and one former outbuilding is now a store.

There once stood a huge oak tree at the corner of Shore and Tuckahoe Roads, but it was cut down around 1968, about the time that the South Shore automobile dealership was built. Many were saddened by the loss of this landmark.

It is no surprise that many younger residents have no idea just how many farms once existed in the township, particularly in the village of Marmora. Stables were quite numerous (one large one was across the street from the Stratton and Collins stores, used by younger residents who rode horses to get around.

It is hard for longtime township residents to drive through Marmora and try to remember what used to be located where. So much has changed in the last 40 to 50 years, but Marmora is still one of the beloved villages of the township.

The Amos Corson house and farm stand today on Randolph Boulevard in Marmora. This photograph was taken in the 1920s, as evidenced by the 1920 Ford Model T Tudor sedan in the driveway by the house. The extent of farmland in Marmora at this time is clearly seen. (Courtesy of HPSUT.)

Today, Clayton Marina on Thirty-fourth Street is a bustling marina. This early 1950s photograph shows no large cabin cruisers, yachts, or even speedboats, as can be seen today. This was just the beginning of what became a huge and profitable business. Carol Collins's brother Arthur worked there for years as a teenager. (Courtesy of Carol Collins.)

This is a photograph of the original Collins-Watchko family house in Marmora. The family had moved from Palermo, where Arthur Collins Sr. had lived. Chrissie Watchko is standing behind the house near the separate kitchen building. Since kitchens frequently caused devastating fires, many homeowners had them built separately from the house. (Courtesy of Carol Collins.)

Trinity Methodist Church was built in 1869. This building replaced the Willet's meetinghouse, built in 1836. It cost $3,700 to erect and was incorporated in 1870 as the Beesley's Point Methodist Episcopal Church and called Trinity. A newer, larger Methodist church was built nearby in 1980, and the Seventh-Day Adventist Church rented the older building for a time. (Courtesy of Curtis Corson Jr.)

Farming was still the principal occupation in Upper Township into the 1930s, as evidenced by this farming family of Marmora proudly looking over a prized calf. Perhaps the calf was to be entered in a competition at the county fair or was recently bought or sold. (Courtesy of Carol Collins.)

Wayside Village in Marmora was once a large farm owned by Fendall Smith. The farm remained until the mid-1960s, when it was sold. The house moved to Stagecoach Road, and the property was developed in the early 1970s. The old pump house is now an ice cream shop. (Courtesy of the *Upper Township Gazette*.)

The popular E.A. Stratton Store and post office was owned by Edgar Stratton of Beesley's Point. Stratton operated the store and Esso gas station with his wife. The post office is to the left of the store. This photograph was taken with Stratton and his wife posing out front. The entire building was moved back sometime in the 1930s in order to widen Route 9. (Courtesy of HPSUT.)

After Edgar Stratton owned the store and gas station, it was purchased by the Getty family (Getty was the subsequent postmaster). It then went through two more hands. Owned briefly by the Clayton family, it was sold to Cody Letsinger, who ran the store as seen here. The post office was moved across the street on the opposite corner. Cody's is now the site of a large chain gas station and convenience store. (Courtesy of HPSUT.)

The Collins Store in Marmora was just south of Stratton's Store on Shore Road. This wintertime photograph was taken in the late 1930s when Collins sold Amoco gasoline and the store was a popular ice cream and snack stop. The building is now occupied by Kirk's Pizza. (Courtesy of Carol Collins.)

The Collins family continued to operate the store even when Arthur Sr. was called to serve his country during World War II. This 1945 photograph is of his son Johnny S. Collins, born in 1940. He is wearing his father's campaign hat in front of the store by the Breyer's ice cream sign. Arthur Collins Sr. had come home from the war. (Courtesy of Carol Collins.)

The Coast Guard Auxiliary of Upper Township is pictured here early in World War II. There are several notable people. At far left in the back row is Arthur P. Collins Sr., and seventh from left in the back row is Edgar Young Corson. At far right in the front row is Ralph Clayton Sr. (Courtesy of Carol Collins.)

This interesting photograph from the 1950s shows Marmora resident Arthur S. Collins Jr. as a teenager taking a photograph through the side of the old Thirty-fourth Street Bridge. Note the house in the background. It was occupied by bridge keeper Richard Vinacomb. (Courtesy of Carol Collins.)

The Collins Store is busy on a summer afternoon in downtown Marmora. The awnings over two windows and on the tanker truck read, "Now: Air Conditioned." The store is now the home of Kirk's Pizza. (Courtesy of Carol Collins.)

Horseback riding was popular in Marmora and throughout the 10 villages of Upper Township. Before teenagers had cars, nearly all teens and older children in Upper Township rode their horses wherever they needed to be. There once was a large horse stable right across from the Collins Store that was used by many in the area. In this 1936 photograph, Billy Sapp and Anna Collins pose in front of the store. (Courtesy of Carol Collins.)

Downtown Marmora in the 1940s was the local business center, and for many people today, it still is. It was were groceries and gasoline could be bought and sodas and ice cream treats could be enjoyed. Even though Rural Free Delivery was established for farm families in 1896, most people still picked up their mail at the post office, located on the southeast corner. (Courtesy of Carol Collins.)

Before the Tuckahoe Academy School and the Palermo School were designated to be sold or torn down, the township had decided to build a new elementary school in Marmora on Tuckahoe Road. This is a photograph of the new Upper Township Elementary School soon after it opened in 1953. Originally, the school taught first through sixth grade. (Courtesy of Carol Collins.)

Three

PALERMO

The origin of this village's name remains unknown, unless one of the early settlers knew about the capital of Sicily!

Palermo, just south of Marmora along Shore Road, is bordered by the current Pine Hill trailer park, about a mile north of Church Road, Hope Corson Road to the south, the marshes and the Garden State Parkway to the east, and Tuckahoe Road and Cedar Swamp Creek to the west. The village is only a three mile stretch, and its isolation kept its population low. In fact, the 1910 census lists the total population of Palermo at just 80 people. It was once described by *History of Upper Township* contributor Anthony Butler as "isolated from both east and west."

But there is much history along this stretch of Shore Road, reflected in the variety and styles of houses along Route 9. Several were built in the 1700s; one of them was likely a stagecoach stop. Butler wrote, "under colonial legislation, any home was obliged to furnish room and board for the traveler and care for his horse."

John and Peter Corson arrived in Corson's Inlet and came to the mainland, building a "cave" as their living quarters until they could build a house. The cave was known as Corson's Cellar and the creek became known as Corson's Creek, but it was all part of what was once the Stephen Young plantation, which stretched through to Petersburg and the Great Cedar Swamp.

In 1762, Joseph Corson and others were authorized to build a toll bridge over Cedar Swamp Creek, but there is no record of a bridge built until 1834. The bridge stimulated a surge in building, and numerous homes were constructed along Shore Road between the 1840s and 1860s. By 1840, the population of Upper Township had risen to 1,217, including Palermo.

The only church in Palermo is the Second Cape May Baptist Church, built in 1853. Located on the east side of Seashore Road in its earliest days as a meetinghouse in 1770, it was later moved to the west side and later razed, so that the newer, larger church with a bell tower could be built in 1853. The church cemetery remains on the east side of the road.

The next major growth period took place in the 1880s on each side of the railroad tracks that led to Ocean City. Palermo opened its first post office in 1872. The first postmaster was James S. Willets, and the last was Seth Corson in 1893, when the post office closed. It was Corson who supervised its merger with Marmora's post office not long after it had opened in 1890.

Numerous homes and inexpensive and efficient bungalows were built after World War I.

There were few businesses in Palermo, but Curtis Corson Sr. owned and operated the Palermo general store there until 1935. It was very popular through the 1920s. The store even sold gasoline. Corson owned his own delivery trucks and used them to pick up and deliver goods around the area. The post office was also located there, attached to their home, as was a dry goods store operated by Corson's wife, Carrie.

The next large growth period for Palermo was in the 1950s and 1960s. In the 1950s, the Palermo Air Force Station on the east side of Shore Road was expanded as a result of the Cold War. There was a large community of Air Force personnel there operating a radar station. The many buildings on the station included a chapel built in the late 1950s. This facility remained open through the late 1970s. It is now the site of the Osprey Point community.

Shore Road was the major artery through Palermo, but it was the construction of the Garden State Parkway that brought even more people to the sleepy village. The parkway opened in 1954, and the southbound lanes were diverted over 100 feet to go around the 300-year-old Shoemaker holly tree, which still stands today in the picnic area built by the parkway.

Taxes in Upper Township were low, and this created great interest in moving to communities like Palermo, but the devastating 1962 nor'easter that hit the shore communities like Ocean City and Sea Isle City spurred an interest in many for a move to the relative safety of the mainland.

The creation of the casino industry in 1977 brought the latest surge in growth. Upper Township became a large bedroom community due to the number of casino workers who needed easy access to the Garden State Parkway to get to work. Palermo changed from a quiet, rural area of farms, virgin timberland, and a modest number of homes, to a busy Shore Road thoroughfare.

In 1816, there was a very cold summer as a result of a volcanic eruption on the other side of the world. Palermo and all of Cape May County experienced frost from June through September, as recorded in the diary of Jeremiah Leaming. There were sheets of ice on ponds in July and August. Many Cape May farmers abandoned their farms and moved to the Ohio Valley, which had seen a boom due to the Northwest Ordinance settlements in Ohio, in the face of this weather crisis.

Another weather event that affected the entire northeast coast was the "Blizzard of '88," also known as the "Great White Hurricane." The east coast from Maine to the Chesapeake Bay was paralyzed by the storm. Snowfalls of up to 60 inches were reported in New Jersey, with sustained winds of 45 mph and snowdrifts up to 50 feet. Railroads and telegraphs were all shut down and early telephone lines became ineffective. People across the northeast were confined to their homes for over a week. This must have been difficult for rural folks who did not have the tools or heavy equipment to dig out. Municipalities in those days did not provide road clearing services, so the local towns were essentially buried with impassable roads for weeks.

Palermo is a beautiful and pleasant three miles down Shore Road, but there are treasures to see, such as the Cameron Wildlife Sanctuary, now part of the county park system. From this property, sand and soil were once removed to build first the railroad beds at the turn of the 20th century and later the Garden State Parkway. This created numerous freshwater ponds, which are now filled with wildlife. Older Palermo residents recall swimming in these ponds in the 1940s.

Palermo is also home to the Friendship School, one of the first public schools in the township, built around 1830. Restoration of this historic building was started during the US bicentennial in 1976 and finished in 1983. Other historic buildings along Shore Road in Palermo are the original Palermo Elementary School, next door to the Friendship School and now a private preschool, and Mechanics Hall, now a real estate office.

Palermo also once had its own busy railroad station, but that is long gone, now located in Historic Wheaton Village.

This 1907 photograph shows the Seashore Road birthplace of former Upper Township businessman and mayor Arthur P. Collins. He was the owner of the Collins Store and photography shop through the 1950s, served on the township committee, and was elected mayor of Upper Township in the 1950s. (Courtesy of Carol Collins.)

Palermo's Pennsylvania–Reading Seashore Line station operated through the 1960s. This photograph was taken in the 1970s before it was moved to Wheaton Village and restored. (Courtesy of Karen Behr.)

The Palermo General Store was started and owned by Jesse S. Corson, then owned by his son Curtis Edward Corson and later his grandson Curtis Townsend Corson Sr. The store, as well as Palermo's post office, was on the left side of the house. Curtis Edward Corson's wife, Carrie Corson, helped operate the post office. Note the gas pumps out front. The Corson family sold the store in 1935 and moved to the Townsend family's house and farm in Seaville, where farming became Curtis Sr.'s principal occupation. (Courtesy of Curtis Corson Jr.)

Palermo General Store owner Curtis Edward Corson and son Curtis Townsend Corson Sr. stand in front of a Dodge delivery van; their other delivery vehicle was a Model T truck. The photograph was taken in the 1920s. (Courtesy of Curtis Corson Jr.)

Pictured with his pet crow, Curtis Townsend Corson Sr. is standing out behind the Palermo General Store. The photograph was taken in the late 1910s. (Courtesy of Curtis Corson Jr.)

This building was the lodge of the Junior Order United American Mechanics on North Shore Road in Palermo. It was built in the late 19th century and remains standing today as a real estate office. (Courtesy of HPSUT.)

The Friendship School in Palermo was built in the 1830s and is typical of schools of that time. Beginning in 1976, it was restored by the township and members of the Historical Preservation Society of Upper Township. The township owns the building, but it is supervised by the HPSUT. (Courtesy of Joan Berkey.)

The Palermo School, built in the 1890s, was used by the township as a public school and taught through the sixth grade until 1953, when the new elementary school was opened. Some older Tuckahoe residents still remember coming to this school all the way from Tuckahoe. It was vacant for many years, but since the 1980s, it has housed a preschool. (Courtesy of Carol Collins.)

This is a charming picture of four schoolchildren with their teacher standing near the Palermo School, which is out of the photograph, to the right, along Seashore Road. The teacher is Rebecca Collins, and the children are, from left to right, LeRoy Wills, John Vizzard, Laura Edmonds, and her younger sister. (Courtesy of Barbara Horan.)

This is the Palermo School class photograph from 1944. From left to right are (first row) Peggy Gandy, Jo Ann Dailey, Betty Ann Young, Jeanne Clayton, Betty Lou Sapp, Ralph Clayton, Conrad Lea, and Jerry Beebe; (second row) Rosemary Pashley, Barbara Gandy, Martha Jeffries, Doris Brandenberger, Laurabelle Crain, Helen Shoonhoff, Louise Dailey, Lois Young, and Louise Brown. Schools like this were frequently one-room schoolhouses with the teacher teaching multiple grades throughout the year. Gradually, Upper Township used these smaller village schools as grade-specific schools. (Courtesy of Barbara Horan.)

The Greek Revival–style Second Cape May Baptist Church was built in 1853. The original church (meetinghouse) was built on land donated to the Anabaptists by Jeremiah Edwards and was finished in 1770. It originally stood across the street on the east side of Shore Road. The cemetery remains on the east side of the road. (Courtesy of Joan Berkey.)

Here is a charming winter picture taken in Palermo around 1920. The sledders are, from left to right, Johnnie Vizzard, Curtis Townsend Corson Sr., and Chick Cossaboone, all about 8 to 10 years old. (Courtesy of Curtis Corson Jr.)

With the onset of the Cold War, the Defense Department reinforced existing World War II coastal Air Force stations and added additional ones. Upper Township had a station in Palermo, complete with a radar tower. It was home to the 770th Aircraft Control & Warning Squadron. Petersburg resident Eugene "Sarge" Radecki was stationed there. This sign was along Seashore Road. The area is now the Osprey Point community. (Courtesy of Michael Houdart.)

This is the pedestal for the radar tower at the Palermo Air Force Station at the time of its dismantling in the late 1970s. No trace of it remains, and the area, once overgrown, was first used by the township for recreation ballfields but was eventually sold for the Osprey Point housing development. (Courtesy of the Cape May County Historical and Genealogical Museum.)

This photograph, taken in about 1957–1958, at the peak of the Cold War, shows the men of the 770th AC&W Squadron turned out for the dedication of the new chapel about to be built on the grounds of the Air Force station. Note both the radar tower in the back and the newer 1956 and 1957 cars parked in front. (Courtesy of Michael Houdart.)

This 1963 photograph of the Pennsylvania–Reading Seashore Line station at Palermo shows that it is at the end of its usefulness. By this time, the station was essentially abandoned and in disrepair. Soon, it was sold off to Wheaton Village. (Courtesy of HPSUT.)

Four

SEAVILLE

The southern border of the township (with Dennis Township) is DeVaul's Run, a short creek near the surveyor family's property. The northern border is Cannon Road, and to the west, it is Route 50 and Corson's Tavern Road. On the east, the border is Ludlam Sound.

Ocean View, once a part of Upper Township (and the home of Upper Township's founder, John Townsend), was separated from Upper Township in 1872 when Ocean View was granted its own post office and was later absorbed into Dennis Township. Ironically, today, all of Seaville and parts of Palermo are incorporated into the Ocean View zip code, 08230, since Seaville no longer has its own post office.

The area was founded in the 1840s by Corsons, and by the 1840s there were 52 families with the name of Corson living in Upper Township, along with Leamings, Baners, Gandys, and Spicers. The early occupations were many and varied, with most employed as sea captains, seamen, whalers, oystermen, clammers, shippers, and boatbuilders. On land, there were framers, hunters, and trappers.

Located on South Shore Road is the Seaville Quaker Meetinghouse. This house of worship was built around 1726 after the Quakers created their regular monthly meeting in 1702. This meetinghouse is significant in that it is not only the oldest Quaker meetinghouse in New Jersey, but also the oldest house of worship continuously used in the state. Quakers were among the first to migrate to Cape May County in the late 1600s, and most settled in Upper Township, which at the time included most of Dennis Township. The meeting has been laid down more than once over the years. It was revived once in 1871 after being used briefly as a school for Upper Township children and once again in the late 1930s. Finally, it was revived in the late 1950s by the Asa Colson family.

Seaville Methodist Episcopal Church on the west side of Shore Road was built on land owned by Zebulon Townsend and his wife, Anthea Corson, in the mid-19th century. The building contract was given to Peter Corson for $1,800 in 1857, which amounts to about $50,000 today. The church was completed and dedicated in 1858. In 1908, an addition was made and included a classroom and library on the second floor, a vestibule, and belfry with bell. In 1921, a social hall was built across the street; however, in 1965, the building was moved across the street to be connected to the church with a breezeway. Tombstones of the Townsend family were moved to the Seaville Methodist Church Cemetery from a spot near Magnolia Lake. In 1972, Abbie Townsend Kaufmann donated land for the stones to be moved to a safer area.

The corner of Routes 9 and 50, even now a bustling commercial intersection, was once the business section of the village. It was called Marshall's Corner, so named because the Marshall Brothers, James Ludlam Marshall and Ellis Hughes Marshall, owned stores there. Sadly, no trace remains today of the original Marshall's Corner structures.

Amos Corson once owned a tavern in the building at the junction of New Bridge and Shore Roads, hence the name of the parallel road to Route 9, Corson's Tavern Road. A blacksmith shop was once on the opposite (east) side of the road, which operated though the 1930s. Thomas Sharp operated a general store in Seaville between the Thomas and John Sharp houses. Dr. Leaming had his dentist office in a building on the property of Joseph Morris on the east side of Shore Road, the northeast corner of Wright's Lane. The first post office in Seaville opened in 1849 and was once located in the Brinton Jacob Corson house on the east side of Old Seashore Road. It ceased operation in 1915 when it was moved to Ocean View.

The Batchelor house, once located on the median of the Garden State Parkway before it was moved after the construction of the parkway, was one of Seaville's earliest homes. It was built around 1790 and was first provided by Amos Corson as a bunkhouse for his woodcutters. The house was bought by Corson's heirs in 1844. Later, it was owned by a Mr. Batchelor and was eventually occupied by members of the Butler family. Still standing in the 1950s on the median of the Garden State Parkway, it was later moved to Cape May Courthouse and then to Smithville.

The Curlew Bay Club, named after its visiting bird hunters, was formerly the home of Capt. Charles Wright of the Coast Guard. The John Townsend house, located across from Magnolia Lake on Shore Road, is now in Ocean View but was once located in what was then Upper Township. The house was not moved, the borders were changed. John Townsend was the founder of Upper Township in 1798.

The Philadelphia & Reading Railroad crossed Shore Road between Katherine Avenue and Hope Corson Road and went on to Strathmere. The tiny Seaville railroad station was octagonal and included a freight house, horse track, and private sidetrack used by the sand plant.

Peter Corson operated a wind gristmill on his farm in 1820. It was on Shore Road near the original US Air Force radar station. In 1820, Jesse Springer erected a gristmill for Thomas Gandy Sr. between the road and the meadow on the land of Z.T. Gandy in the back of the site of the old Texaco gas station.

The schools of Seaville have an interesting history, with the Quaker meetinghouse actually used as a schoolhouse in the mid-1700s. Eventually, in the late 19th century, Seaville had its own one-room schoolhouse, heated by a coal stove, housing grades one through five. This building is still standing today at the end of Kruk Road behind Dino's Diner and is used for storage. Sixth-graders went on to the Petersburg School, and the seventh-graders eventually went on to the brick former high school on Mount Pleasant Avenue in Tuckahoe.

This introduction would not be complete without a mention of the community of Joelfield. In the early 19th century, a small pioneer community of small homes and tilled fields developed on the west side of Corson Tavern Road. As time went by, folks moved away, the homes burned down, and the fields became overgrown into woodlands. Joelfield disappeared. One group of residents in this area was the Wright family. Captain Wright and his grandfather John Wright had a home here. The Cossaboone, Shaw, and Lutz families lived there as well. The houses are long gone, but some of the family names are still known in the township, and those in the know still refer to the area as Joelfield.

The township has been protected by four fire departments, but none had a paid force—all were volunteers. Marmora and Tuckahoe have had fire companies since the early 20th century, but Seaville's was not formed as a cohesive volunteer company until 1964. A 1944 International fire truck was loaned to Seaville and housed in a gas station across the street from the present firehouse. In January 1966, a new firehouse was constructed on Route 50 on land donated by volunteer Curtis Townsend Corson Sr. Sadly, he died fighting a fire in May 1979.

This photograph shows the home of the founder of Upper Township, John Townsend. A banished Quaker from Long Island, he searched for a tolerant religious climate and decided to settle in Cape May County in Upper Precinct. The house, originally a log cabin, was built in 1690. Near the home, he built a mill on what is now Magnolia Lake. Despite no longer being located in Upper Township, the house is too important to the history of the township to not be included in this book. (Courtesy of Barbara Horan.)

The old Baner house on Shore Road was later owned by renowned bird carver Harry Shourd. The Baners were Quakers who belonged to the Seaville Friends Meeting. The house and barn have stood here since the mid-19th century. The barn is currently used as an art studio by the owner. (Courtesy of HPSUT.)

The Seaville Methodist Church was first built in 1858 in the Greek Revival style on land donated by Zebulon Townsend, who died in 1853. The congregation was organized in 1856, and Peter Corson, the lowest bidder, was contracted to build the church for $1,800. The vestibule and belfry shown here were added in 1908. (Courtesy of Curtis Corson Jr.)

This is Seaville Methodist Church's social hall after it was built in 1921 across the street from the church. It was moved across the street in 1964 and attached to the side of the church by a breezeway. (Courtesy of Curtis Corson Jr.)

By the late 1930s, congregants who may have been unable to get to church on Sunday were able to take the Seaville Methodist Church bus. Here is a photograph of the bus and a group of happy passengers. (Courtesy of Lynne Dress.)

The Richard Somers Townsend house was built in the late 19th century on Seashore Road near the Seaville Methodist Church. Townsend was a Civil War veteran and built the house after his return from the war. A front porch was added in 1916. The house was later the home of Abbie Townsend Kaufmann, who sold it and acreage to the church. She died in 1977 at the age of 97. (Courtesy of Lynne Dress.)

Greek immigrant Dino Karayiannias was a popular and respected restaurateur, whose first establishment in Seaville is shown here. In the 1970s, it was near the intersection of Routes 9 and 50. The restaurant was originally known as The Girls' Wayside Kitchen when he purchased it in 1977. He developed it into the very popular Dino's Wayside Kitchen. Dino became well known and beloved for his friendliness and great charity toward the community. This restaurant lasted until a new building was built on Route 50. (Courtesy of Nick Karayiannias.)

Nick Karayiannias, Dino's son, stands on the front steps of the expanded Dino's Seaville Diner, one of the most well-known, favorite dining spots in the area. Upper Township residents have revered this place as well as its creator, Dino, who passed away from cancer in 2007 at age 66. The diner on Route 50 was enlarged and modernized to handle the increased number of patrons, and unfortunately, no photographs exist of the original building. Son Nick carries on his father's proud traditions. (Photograph by the author.)

Nearly every village of Upper Township had its own school, and Seaville was no exception. The Seaville School, located on what is now Kruk Road down the street from Dino's Diner, is still standing but looks nothing like it once did. This school was built in the same architectural design as the Palermo School. Here, students are pictured in 1905. (Courtesy of Harriett Reardon Bailey.)

This house, built by Isaac Baner in the 1860s, is listed on the 1872 Beers map. Baner is also listed in the 1870 census as a 52-year-old boatbuilder living with his wife, Tabitha, and four children. There is a local story that the home was later occupied by one Dr. Blake, but according to Joan Berkey, architectural historian, there is no record of him living in this house, nor any record of a Dr. Blake living in Cape May County in the mid-19th century. (Courtesy of Lynne Dress.)

Robert Carlson's mother in law, Mildred Jordan, stands behind the Route 50 sign just in front of her son-in-law's establishment, Bob's Service Station and Luncheonette about where the front garden and sign for Dino's Diner are located today. (Courtesy of Leonard R. Carlson.)

Robert Carlson, the 17-year-old owner of Bob's Service Station and Luncheonette and gas station, stands in front of his establishment, which was located at "the Triangle" in Seaville. The station and store were very popular. At the time this photograph was taken around 1938, gasoline was approximately 22¢ per gallon. (Courtesy of Leonard R. Carlson.)

Here is another photograph of the Seaville School, taken around 1910–1915. The photograph, although torn through the center, is amazingly clear, and one can see the range of ages that existed in schoolhouse at that time. Large hair bows were still popular for girls, and boys, of course, wore knickerbocker pants and high socks. (Courtesy of Harriett Reardon Bailey.)

This is a 1930 photograph of the Horace and Clara Townsend house, originally the Amos Corson house, built in 1828. It was originally a tavern run by Miles Corson, nephew of Amos. He operated the tavern through 1834. The road to South Dennis that starts in front of the former tavern was actually laid out in 1812 and is now known as Corson's Tavern Road. The house became a residence occupied by the Townsends and was later sold. It now houses the popular business Wild Garden Accents. (Courtesy of Lynne Dress.)

The Curlew Bay Club has changed dramatically. The original clubhouse was a sportsmen's clubhouse, like the Stillwell-Chattin house in Beesley's Point, and was used mainly for fishing and hunting expeditions. It resembled a hotel with 10 bedrooms on the second floor and a large dormitory on the third floor. In 1876, its stockholders incorporated the club. By 1890, it passed on to the Charles Wright family, and his descendants still own the hunting club. (Courtesy of HPSUT.)

This photograph is of the Reardon farm, a typical farm along Seashore Road in Seaville, which directly bordered the road. (Courtesy of Harriett Reardon Bailey.)

This previously unknown photograph is of the Seaville railroad station, taken on April 8, 1917. The round shape is unlike most other stations in the area. There is still discussion about whose home sits on the hill in the distance. Nothing is known about the fate of this interesting station. (Courtesy of Lynne Dress.)

The intersection of Seashore Road and Route 50 was once a bustling place of business. This rare photograph shows the businesses at what was once called "Marshall's Corner," located on the east side of Shore Road just south of the current Garden State Parkway south entrance. This row of stores, including a general store, hardware store, and harness shop, was once owned by the wealthy Marshall brothers, James and Ellis. The photograph was taken in about 1899. (Courtesy of Curtis Corson Jr.)

This is the home of Hulda Jordan and her daughter Mildred across from the Reardon farm on Shore Road. Mildred's daughter Ella Jordan married Robert Carlson, the owner of Bob's Service Station on Route 50. (Courtesy of Harriett Reardon Bailey.)

This hand-labeled photograph, taken in the 1930s, is of a farm on Seashore Road. Note the farmer plowing with a horse and steel plow. The furrows go right up to the roadway for maximum growth area of the crop. There are no sidewalks or walkways. (Courtesy of Harriett Reardon Bailey.)

On the 1872 Beers map, this particular Gandy house is listed as being across Seashore Road from the Seaville Quaker Meetinghouse. The home's construction represents the marriage of Anthea Townsend to Jesse Gandy. According to architectural historian Joan Berkey, the house, located on land inherited from her grandfather John Townsend, who died in 1832, was built with a heavy timber frame and posts and beams in about 1833 in the vernacular Federal style. (Courtesy of the Cape May County Historical and Genealogical Museum.)

This is a previously unpublished photograph of a Peerless steam tractor, made in Pennsylvania, chugging down Route 9 and towing five gravel wagons as they pave Route 9. The tractor is passing in front of the old Thomas Gandy house, which was later occupied by the Argoe family, as well as members of the Curtis Corson family. (Courtesy of Colleen Argoe-Super.)

This is a turn-of-the-century photograph of the original Batchelor house, built in 1727–1729. It was occupied later by the Butler family and then the Stebbins family. From left to right are Mark Stebbins, Bill Stebbins (infant at base of the tree), Elizabeth Stebbins, Maggie Stebbins (born 1880), and family friend Joe Seddon. (Courtesy of Grace and Tom Garrity.)

This is what remained of the Batchelor house at the time of the construction of the Garden State Parkway through Seaville in 1952–1954. Parkway workmen did not destroy the house, but rather left it standing on the grassy, wooded median. They placed a sign on the side that read, "This Ol' House." It was later moved to Cape May Courthouse and then to Cold Spring Village where it later collapsed. (Courtesy of Grace and Tom Garrity.)

This Seaville farm photograph is of Curtis Edward Corson, Curtis Corson Jr.'s grandfather, with his hired farmhand Bill in front of a wagon filled with logs destined for the sawmill or, judging by their size and girth, to be made into fence posts. The photograph was taken in the 1930s. Curtis Edward Corson grew many kinds of vegetables on his farm; the predominant one was lima beans. (Courtesy of Curtis Corson Jr.)

Curtis Townsend Corson Sr., Curtis Corson Jr.'s father, stands proudly dressed up with his 1935 Lincoln sedan. He is in front of the Townsend family home, which he had recently moved into. After his return from the Civil War, Eugene Townsend built this Seaville home. The house still stands on Seashore Road, has been beautifully restored, and is owned by Curtis Corson Jr.'s son Somers Corson. (Courtesy of Curtis Corson Jr.)

The Seaville Friends Meetinghouse, located on South Shore Road, was built in about 1726–1727. The original congregation met in Friends' homes when it was formed as a monthly meeting in 1702. The building was constructed in Beesley's Point and moved to Seaville around 1763–1764. This is not only the oldest Quaker meetinghouse in New Jersey, but also the oldest house of worship continuously used in the state. (Courtesy of the Cape May County Historical and Genealogical Museum.)

In 1708, Thomas Gandy built his house on a large parcel of land purchased from the West New Jersey Society. He emigrated from Long Island and settled here in 1694. His descendant George Gandy was a Civil War veteran. This 1940s photograph was taken when the Argoe family owned the house. The building had been continuously lived in through the 1970s. It is now owned by Our Children's Country Place Preschool. (Courtesy of Colleen Argoe-Super.)

The Reeves-Iszard-Godfrey House, formerly the Philip Godfrey House, is the most architecturally significant house extant in Cape May County, according to architectural historian Joan Berkey. Built around 1695, it has all the hallmarks of first-period heavy timber frame, post-and-beam construction. It is the best-preserved example of this building technique in the state of New Jersey. It was restored and lived in by beloved HPSUT member and historian Lew Albrecht and his wife, Jean, who still lives there today. (Courtesy of HPSUT.)

This is a rare view of early Shore Road. The back reads, "Shows walking path in front of Rising Sun Inn with Laura Devaul Speer, wife of Wm. Speer. Lucien Eddy's home directly in back of her was built @1904. The Justus B. Crandall house at the left was built @1880 when the church property was sold to Homer Eddy & wife Edith Townsend. The house was moved to cor. of Rising Sun Inn to Boyce Lane. to make ground available for the bank." (Courtesy of Barbara Horan.)

School buses have not always been yellow, as evidenced by this wonderful late 1920s photograph taken in Seaville. The two youngsters outside of the bus are Curtis Townsend Corson Sr. (left) and Chick Cossaboone. (Courtesy of Curtis Corson Jr.)

The border between Upper Township and Dennis Township has been long debated but recently put to rest. This turn-of-the-century photograph shows that exact border. Looking north up Seashore Road are the marshes and DeVaul's Run. This creek is the official border between the two townships. (Courtesy of Colleen Argoe-Super.)

Five

GREENFIELD

Greenfield was once known as Sacktown, named after the David Sack family, one of the village's earliest settlers. Sack arrived in the early 19th century with his wife, Hannah, and started a farm. Most early settlers were farmers, weavers, and carpenters.

William Tullner, who wrote about Greenfield in the 1989 *A History of Upper Township and Its Villages*, stated that, by the late 1800s, the local farmers made good use of Cedar Swamp Creek as a waterway, transporting their crops to Longport and Atlantic City by flat-bottomed boats called market boats. One such boat was owned by Edward Burley and Milton Godfrey of Tuckahoe. Their boat, typical of those of the day, could carry 1,200 baskets of produce to the Boatman's Market in Atlantic City.

Greenfield, the smallest of the 10 villages, is bounded on the east by Cedar Swamp Creek and on the south by, more than likely, Seaville's Katharine Avenue. It is intersected by Tyler Road, which runs to Tuckahoe Road, and Route 50, which runs directly to Tuckahoe. Cedar Bridge forms the northern boundary, and the western boundary is the Cape May Wildlife Refuge.

Another early settler was David Gandy, born in 1816. He was listed as a weaver in the 1860 census. His son John Wesley Gandy was a preacher and a farmer. That same census includes Champion Corson and his wife, Mary, whose farm was across from the Sack farm on New Bridge Road. Tullner writes that the 1872 map shows the properties of carpenter Youngs Corson and farmer Kinsey Corson, just north of the Champion Corson farm. Another neighbor was Rachel French, whose older son was a waterman and whose younger son was a farmer.

So, when did Sacktown become Greenfield? According to legend, when the railroad to Sea Isle passed though in 1893, a small station was built. The surrounding green fields were plentiful, and thus, the name Greenfield was suggested. Eventually, the name Sacktown just faded away, and the area became widely known as Greenfield.

David Gandy, as one of the earliest settlers, was descended from Thomas Gandy, who came to Cape May County in 1694 as one of the original "whaler yeomen." The Gandy family had been involved in the township's political and community life for many years. John Wesley Gandy, born in 1847, and his wife, Emma Lavinia van Gilder Gandy, were both descended from Cape May County pioneer families. John married Emma in 1872. They raised six children in a home on Tyler Road; today, the home has been restored and is owned by the township and supervised by the Historical Preservation Society of Upper Township. The Gandy house was built in 1815 by Joseph Falkenburge and was in use through 1950. John Wesley Gandy was an interesting man. He was a farmer, minister, constable, and district superintendent of schools. He was also once owner of the Cedar Swamp Meadow Company. Predeceased by his wife, he lived in the house until 1929.

The heirs of Winifred Gandy donated the house and one acre of land on which it stands to the historical society, which preserves it to honor this member of the Gandy family. The house has been restored through the hard work of township residents and dedicated historians like John Siegrist, Lew Albrecht, and Sonia Forry. Sometime later, a period barn was moved to the site and stands there today as part of the farm's outbuildings, including a smokehouse, icehouse, and privy. There is also a working windmill water pump. The Gandy house appears on the 1872 Beers map in the Cape May Historical Society records and in the 1977 Cape May County inventory of historic buildings.

Today, Greenfield is home to several popular stores and businesses along Route 50, the earliest being Frog Hollow bakery. First started by Joe Patterson in 1977 after a move from Ocean City, Frog Hollow Bakery has become legendary for its baked goods, which are only sold from April through October. A popular campground, shops, a restaurant, ice cream stand, and small strip malls also dot Route 50. Many in Greenfield and the surrounding area remember Conrad and Dolly Heiser Deuter and their farm. There, one could buy Christmas trees for a great price and get expert gardening tips.

Years ago, a Wawa store and gas station stood on the corner of Route 50 and Hope Corson Road. The store remained, but the gas pumps were removed some 25 years ago, and they are still missed by locals who enjoyed the convenience of getting a few gallons of inexpensive gas whenever needed. Another convenience store recently took its place, without gas pumps.

There are not quite as many green fields as there once were, but residents of Greenfield would like the reader to know that the village is more than just a Route 50 thoroughfare from Seaville to Tuckahoe. The village continues to grow at the slowest of paces, which suits the residents of Greenfield just fine.

Built in approximately 1791, this house originally belonged to Phoebe and Joseph Corson Jr. Joseph Corson Sr. willed the land the house sits on as part of "a place called Fast Landing on the southeasterly side of Cedar Swamp Creek." The addition to the house that faces Tyler Road was added in the 1850s–1860s. (Courtesy of HPSUT.)

The Frog Hollow bakery was once a private residence, built in about 1915 right on Route 50. Businessman Joseph "Joe" Patterson, who had moved from Ocean City to start a bakery, purchased the house and property. He established Frog Hollow in the building in 1971, the first business along that stretch of Route 50. The popular bakery is still open today and is operated by Joe's son Jody and his wife, Debbie Patterson. (Photograph by the author.)

This 1980s photograph shows the soon-to-be-restored John Wesley Gandy farmhouse on Tyler Road. Members of the dedicated restoration crew seen here are, from left to right, James Siegrist, Paul Kuhnle, Sonia Forry, Ned McDermott, and Reynolds Schmidt. (Courtesy of Sonia Forry.)

The Gandy Farmhouse on Tyler Road was restored in about 2005. It is a good example of post-and-beam construction, according to Joan Berkey. In 1815, Joseph Falkenburge built it as a tenant farmer house on land purchased originally by Henry Young from the West Jersey Society in 1725. Later purchased in 1878, it is named for John Wesley Gandy, a farmer, minister, school superintendent, and manager of the Cedar Swamp Meadows Company. He lived here until his death in 1929. (Courtesy of Sonia Forry.)

Six

PETERSBURG

Petersburg has often been considered the heart of Upper Township, and not just because of its location. The label seems fitting, because the seat of government, the municipal court, the middle school, and the county library branch are all now located here.

Petersburg was once known as Littleworth because those who first settled the area considered the land of "little worth." The village is bordered on the east by Cedar Swamp Creek, on the north by Middletown (eventually part of Tuckahoe), on the far west by Steelmantown, and on the south by Greenfield. Exact borders are difficult to determine, but roadways and waterways make it easier. The Dennisville-Petersburg Road, the first officially authorized and constructed road in the area, was laid out by surveyors in 1798 and ran from Dennis Creek to Littleworth. The road was opened for public use on December 1, 1798.

David Corson and James Townsend, along with 10 other inhabitants of Upper Precinct, petitioned the state assembly for a road between the houses of Parmenas Corson in Seaville and Job Young, running north and west and crossing over Cedar Swamp Creek to the Cumberland County line. The Tuckahoe Seaville Road was built 40 feet wide and opened in December 1801. Tyler Road was petitioned for by Joseph Corson and others. Surveying for this road was started on November 17, 1818, and it opened in August 1819. The Tuckahoe–Beesley's Point Road was laid out in 1820. Its course changed in 1857 and again in 1906 when it was widened.

Petersburg's first settlers were along Cedar Swamp Creek, which was much larger in the 18th century. The creek flowed into the Tuckahoe River and offered easy access to the bays, ocean, and woodlands for the lumber needed to build homes and operate the sawmills and grist mills. In the early 18th century, Abraham and John Van Gilder came by sloop from Long Island, New York, and sailed up the Tuckahoe River to Cedar Swamp Creek. Their father, Johannes Van Gilder, had settled in New Amsterdam. At a place where the Upper Bridge would later be built, they lived in an Indian "cave" until they could buy land from the West Jersey Society and build a home. It was here that the first Van Gilder was born in Cape May County.

Abraham Van Gilder built a log house just west of their landing spot. He wrote, "the land was of little worth," thus naming the area and the eventual village. John van Gilder built a log home close to his brother's house, and together they became land owners. Cornelius Corson was a private in the Cape May militia who bought property from Jeremiah Van Gilder in 1787 and built a frame and brick house near where the old Methodist church was later built in 1853. Sadly, the home was torn down in the 1930s. Cornelius married Sarah Corson, and one of their six sons, Peter, built the old brick house that stands across from the church.

The first Petersburg school was deeded in 1814, known as the Franklin School, and began classes in 1820. Money for the school was raised by subscription. The Franklin School's first teacher was

Elias Corson, who worked a seven-hour day for 48 days at $30, but paid his own board. Tuition was three cords of wood for each student. As an incentive for better students, a fourth cord would be supplied. A new, second school was built in 1871, with an addition added in 1909, and is still standing as a private home.

In 1825, Thomas Van Gilder established a store at the intersection of the Petersburg-Dennisville Road and the Tuckahoe–Beesley's Point Road. It was in business until 1905. It was in this store that the post office was located from 1862 to 1885 and again from 1909 to 1913.

Local landmarks and businesses included the Upper Bridge, built in 1788; the Old Landing Wharf, where schooners took on cedar "shooks" (shakes) for barrel making and probably for roofing; Meadow Bank, an old tidal saw mill built on Mackey Place by John Mackey between 1740 and 1757; Smith's Mill, a wheelwright and paint shop and, by 1892, a saw mill; Creamer's Mill, built in 1800 on 118 acres by Cedar Swamp Creek; California Mills, built in 1846 and designed by local entrepreneur Peter Hoff for Thomas van Gilder and used as a gristmill and sawmill before it was destroyed in an 1895 fire; the Corner Store, built in 1834 and first established by Peter Corson and Harrison Westcott; the Philadelphia Store, built by Thaddeus van Gilder as a millinery, later a grocery store run by Thomas Homan, Cornelius Corson, and Elizabeth Hess, destroyed in a storm in 1880 and later rebuilt; and the Redman's Lodge on old Tuckahoe Road, a meeting place for men who belonged to the Improved Order of Red Men Wendagoes Tribe No. 91. They first met in a house and moved to the van Gilder's store upstairs until the lodge could be built. The lodge still stands today as a private home.

The solitary church in Littleworth was the Wesley Methodist Episcopal Church. It was organized in 1831, and initially the congregants met in members' homes. Elias Corson and nine other Corson families along with the Godfreys, Mickels, and a Mr. Peterson formed the initial group, which later organized to build the Wesley Meetinghouse in 1853. It was built by Peter Corson for $3,200. In 1967, a school section was added with a kitchen and dining area in the basement. Today, the Petersburg Methodist Church is an active and vibrant congregation.

The name of the town was changed to Petersburgh (the "h" was later dropped) just before the Civil War to honor its favorite son, Peter Corson, who was one of the most important men in the township: the first postmaster, local builder, and a prominent Methodist. The Petersburg post office was established February 8, 1949. Previously, Tuckahoe was the post office for the area.

By 1869, Petersburg had two shipyards, two sawmills, a gristmill, three stores, three shops, and about 400 inhabitants. Thomas van Gilder built a sawmill and later a gristmill on Cedar Swamp Creek in 1846, both designed and built by local entrepreneur and genius Peter Hoff. According to the 1913 *History of Petersburg*, the original railroad in Upper Township ran from Middletown to Cedar Swamp Creek, crossing the Dennisville Road where Killdeer Hill Road branches off. The route was changed at the insistence of the residents. By 1894, the Ocean City branch of the Philadelphia and Reading Railroad was constructed, and by 1897 ran from Cedar Springs through the Palermo Station and on to Ocean City.

It is obvious now that what was once of "little worth" is certainly more aptly named Petersburg.

This is a fine photograph of the historic Capt. Allen and Sarah Corson house, built in 1818. Allen was in the Cape May Independent Regiment as a lieutenant in 1818, and again as captain in 1822. He was also justice of the peace from 1831 to 1835. By the time of the 1872 Beers map, the house was occupied by Allen and Sarah's children Rachel, Victoria, Allen Jr., and Pennington. (Courtesy of Lynne Dress.)

This is a view of Fast Landing at the foot of the old Littleworth Bridge near Young's boatyard on Cedar Swamp Creek. Stephen Young's home and store, built around 1813, can be seen. According to Joan Berkey, "The shorter two-story section was the original store and the three westernmost bays of the taller section were the original parts of the house that Young built." The view today across the creek would be of Holt's Boat Works. (Courtesy of Paul Loveland III.)

The original part of the Charles and Martha Caldwell house, also known as Arbutus Hill (the section at far left), was built in 1886. This smaller home, a farmhouse on 100 acres, had three generations of family members living in just two bedrooms. The 1900 census lists Charles, age 42; Martha, 38; six children aged 12 to 3, and Martha's father, Peter Hoff. A local entrepreneur and mill builder, Hoff is buried in Petersburg Methodist Church cemetery. (Courtesy of Joan Berkey.)

This is a rare photograph of what is believed to be the Petersburg School choir in 1889. The teacher is Mr. Mickels. Note that all the girls have the same outfit, which is interesting because no public school students wore uniforms in those days. The photograph is labeled "Christmas Eve, 1889." (Courtesy of the Dennisville Historical Museum.)

1908 - Harry Butler

Harry Butler, Grace Garrity's uncle, was a local huckster (a person who took vegetables, eggs, and notions from farmers to market). Butler was a popular man in Petersburg. This photograph was taken on Perry Road, and the house in the background was on the corner of Route 50. (Courtesy of Grace and Tom Garrity.)

During World War II, airplane-spotting stations were common in coastal areas. This one was on Route 610 in Petersburg near the train tacks that went through town. Note the electrical panel box by the tracks. (Courtesy of Grace and Tom Garrity.)

A mother walks her infant in a carriage on a dirt sidewalk in this 1910 photograph of what is now known as Route 610. The view is looking east (toward Route 50) around the corner from the Petersburg Methodist Church. Most roads like this were unpaved at the time. (Courtesy of Grace and Tom Garrity.)

In 1918, the Butler brothers, along with other local men of Petersburg, signed up to fight in the Great War. The recruiter may have just given them cigars to seal the deal. The men include Isaac, Harry (in uniform), Robert, William, and Frank Butler—all uncles of Grace Garrity. These men must have enlisted just before the armistice in November 1918 because they never saw action. (Courtesy of Grace and Tom Garrity.)

Smith's General Store was on the corner of Routes 610 and 50 in Petersburg. Originally, it was Peter Corson's general store for many years. The building still stands today as a private residence. (Courtesy of Lynne Dress.)

Boschee's Syrup was a very popular elixir and was used for all kinds of ailments; around 1910, it and other patent medicines were sold everywhere, including general stores and pharmacies. Some medicines, which at the time were unregulated by the government, contained large quantities of alcohol and occasionally stronger ingredients such as laudanum. This flyer from the Van Gilder general store in Petersburgh—before the "H" was dropped— was widely distributed. (Courtesy of HPSUT.)

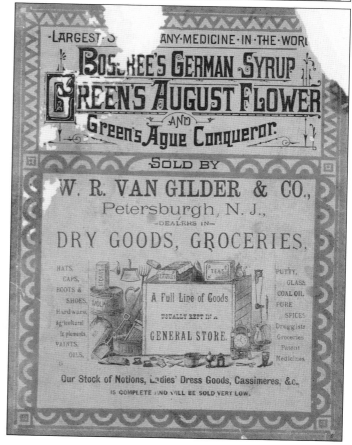

·LARGEST· ⸱ ANY·MEDICINE·IN·THE·WORL

BOSCHEE'S GERMAN SYRUP

GREEN'S AUGUST FLOWER

—AND—

Green's Ague Conqueror.

SOLD BY

W. R. VAN GILDER & CO.,

Petersburgh, N. J.,

—DEALERS IN—

DRY GOODS, GROCERIES,

HATS,
CAPS,
BOOTS &
SHOES,
Hardware,
Agricultural
Implements,
PAINTS,
OILS,
&c.

A Full Line of Goods
USUALLY KEPT IN A
GENERAL STORE.

PUTTY,
GLASS,
COAL OIL,
PURE
SPICES,
Druggists
Groceries,
Patent
Medicines

Our Stock of Notions, Ladies' Dress Goods, Cassimeres, &c.,
IS COMPLETE AND WILL BE SOLD VERY LOW.

Petersburg Methodist Church was first built in 1853 by local builder and favorite son Peter Corson, for whom the town was named. The building stands today on the bend on Route 610 and is a popular and widely attended church. The cedar tree is also still growing there. As evidenced by the bicycle, this photograph was probably taken in the 1920s. (Courtesy of Grace and Tom Garrity.)

This c. 1913 photograph shows the students of Petersburg School. The one-room schoolhouse still stands today as a private home on Old Tuckahoe Road. The teacher is unidentified. (Courtesy of Grace and Tom Garrity.)

This is yet another wonderful photograph of the Petersburg School taken a few years earlier. Note the fashions of the day. Boys wore knickerbockers, knee-high socks, and shirts with bow ties, and girls wore cotton dresses with large bows in their hair. Large hair bows were quite popular through the 1910s. Teachers were required to teach children of all ages and grade levels (first through eighth). Kindergarten did not yet exist. (Courtesy of Grace and Tom Garrity.)

Henry Ford's Model T was ubiquitous in the early 20th century. Upper Township was no different than anywhere else. This is a c. 1915 photograph of a 1912–1913 Model T at the Petersburg train station. The date on the license plate (plates were issued every year) is illegible, but this Model T may have been driven by Tuckahoe resident Louise Letsinger's grandfather, who was reportedly the only taxi driver in Upper Township. (Courtesy of Merry and Joe May.)

This photograph, taken during a summer between 1915 and 1920, shows Petersburg's train station. The boy at far left is wearing a white linen suit. Since the previous photograph, the station has expanded and is using an old railcar for storage. (Courtesy of Merry and Joe May.)

This building, located on Route 610 in Petersburg, once housed the Redman's lodge of Upper Township. The Improved Order of Red Men was a private fraternal organization for men, usually businessmen and politicians. Some members of the Wendagoes Tribe No. 91, like those from Ocean City, had to travel long distances to attend meetings at the lodge. Today, this building is a private home. (Courtesy of Grace and Tom Garrity.)

In the 1910s and 1920s, there was a wide variety of gas stations—one Tuckahoe resident recalls about 17 gas stations in Tuckahoe alone. This Sinclair station on the corner of Perry Road and Route 50 was owned by Aimee Barrett and his wife. The sign shows that the price was 21.8¢ per gallon. The original building is gone, but the current owner still has one of the gas pumps. It is currently Dave's Auto Repair of Petersburg. (Courtesy of Grace and Tom Garrity.)

Lucy Regine, a teacher in Upper Township for over 40 years, lived in this house on the old Tuckahoe Road in Petersburg. It was originally built around 1773. Described in Craig's *History of Petersburg* as having been owned by Thaddeus van Gilder in 1872, it was later owned by Neil Regine in the 1930s. According to Joan Berkey, the Van Gilder Store was nearby, as was the post office, and this home was likely a tenant house. (Courtesy of Grace and Tom Garrity.)

This sunny c. 1900 photograph shows the students of Petersburg School—note how many of the children are shading their eyes. The little boy sitting in the first row, second from right, is not wearing shoes. (Courtesy of Barbara Horan.)

Pictured outside their home on the corner of Route 50 and Perry Road is the Butler family at their farm stand in 1940. On the far right, Grace Garrity is selling vegetables she grew with her parents. (Courtesy of Grace and Tom Garrity.)

Seven

TUCKAHOE

Before traveling to Tuckahoe along Route 50, it was necessary to go through the village of Middletown. There are several Upper Township residents alive today who were born in Middletown, but it is no longer a separate village, having long ago been absorbed into Tuckahoe. Middletown was in the area surrounding the intersection of Route 50 and the Tuckahoe Road. At the intersection today is Levari's Seafood & American Grill, which was previously Triton Bar. There was once a Baptist church across the street from the restaurant, but now all that is there are briars and vines.

Local names on the 1872 Beers map include Budd, Buzby, Young, Stevens, Hand, Simpson, and Bailey. D. Bailey had a carpenter's shop and was a shipbuilder at the Corson shipyard in the 1860s. J. Bailey and J. Buzby were farmers. Across the road from D. Bailey's home was the house of J.B. Hess, a wheelwright and wagon maker. That home is still on the east side of Route 50 approaching Tuckahoe.

In the late 1800s, most farmers sent their produce to the Boatman's Market in Atlantic City on their own boats, but as motorized trucks became more popular, they trucked their produce to the wharf in Tuckahoe and had it sent by flatboats.

The McNamara Game Preserve in what was once Middletown was a Civilian Conservation Corps camp during the Great Depression. During World War II, German prisoners of war were kept in the old buildings on the site and were taken out daily to work as farmhands.

The Baptist church is gone, and most buildings that once dotted Middletown have vanished; however, those born in the area, like local Steelmantown resident and longtime historical society member Jerry Bailey, still remember it fondly.

"Where the deer are shy" is just one of the accepted meanings of the Lenni Lenape word *tuckahoe*. Another is that it is named after the wild tuckahoe, a fungus (*Wolfiporia extensa*) that grew in abundance in this area on the roots of certain trees and was collected by the members of the Lenni Lenape tribes.

Whatever the meaning of Tuckahoe, this area was favored by Native Americans for its fishing, hunting, and foraging opportunities. It is no coincidence that this area was also favored by early white settlers. Conditions were perfect for these newcomers. Settlements began on both sides of the river in the late 1600s. By the 19th century, there was North Tuckahoe across the river (later Corbin City) and Williamsburg (the current village of Tuckahoe).

The river was a busy thoroughfare, with businesses flourishing in shipbuilding, bog iron production, and glassmaking. From the mid- to late 19th century, many two-masted schooners were built and launched along the river. Timber was cut from local forests, and iron and nails were supplied from the Aetna iron furnace and foundry farther north at Head of the River.

South Tuckahoe, known as Williamsburg, was probably named for the first postmaster, John Williams, in 1828, but for some reason, the name never stuck. Interestingly, Steelmantown and Middletown are listed in the postal register but not Williamsburg, which signifies that the town was known as such by the locals only.

Before the railroads, stagecoaches were the primary way of traveling far distances. In 1716, a county road was built from Long Bridge to the head of the Tuckahoe River and from there to Gloucester Point. Stagecoaches began to run in about 1770. One of two stage lines, the Tuckahoe Stage ran from Philadelphia to Mays Landing and then to Tuckahoe. The fare was $3.50, which was steep for 1770—about $80 today. The other line, the Bridgeton Stage, ran through the Bayshore towns to Cape Island.

Steam travel came to the area by way of side-wheeler steamships, which could carry passengers to Atlantic City or even Philadelphia. Steam trains came to Tuckahoe in 1893, and a new train station was built there in 1894. Tuckahoe became a critical junction for the railroads. It was an economic boon for the area because the glass factory in Marshallville had closed and jobs were scarce. Tuckahoe became a railroad town, with a repair station for the Reading Railroad Line and the main junction, from which the trains of the Philadelphia and Seashore Railroads fanned out to Cape May seashore communities like Strathmere and Sea Isle City. By 1894, dozens of trains loaded with tourists destined for the shore resorts were traveling through the station. The tourists were nicknamed "shoobies" because many brought their lunches in shoeboxes. The fare was $1, about $25 today. By the 1950s, steam was gradually replaced by diesel, and slowly, the train traffic diminished because of the automobile. By 1982, all train traffic except for fuel trains destined for the B.L. England generating station in Beesley's Point ceased going through Tuckahoe.

Some of the industries that remained in the area included the production of cranberries and silk (a factory on Reading Avenue), canning tomatoes (Diamont canning factory), and boatbuilding (Yank Boat Works). Tuckahoe has lost any aspect of an industrial town, but a train still runs occasionally on the old tracks from Richland to Tuckahoe. The old 1894 Tuckahoe train station is owned by Upper Township, and the Historical Preservation Society of Upper Township uses it as its office. The historical society works with the Cape May Seashore Line for special events. Since the 2019 closing of the B.L. England generating station, trains carrying long lines of coal cars no longer traverse the tracks through Tuckahoe, but Conrail trains still occasionally move through the junction.

There are still some small businesses in town, including antique shops, a bank, diner, funeral parlor, florist shop, coffee shop, cheesecake shop, post office, bike shop, ice cream shop, popular community center, and a skilled volunteer fire department, which was organized in 1927. The single church in town is the Tuckahoe Methodist Church, first built in 1839. A fire destroyed the building in 1939, but a new church was constructed that still stands today; however, its steeple has been replaced twice since 1940.

The downtown area has recently been completely updated and modernized, with a repaved Main Street (Route 50), sidewalks, curbing, and beautiful cast-iron streetlights. Tuckahoe residents are loyal to their village, and the river, once bustling with business traffic, is now used exclusively for recreational activities like boating, swimming, riding Jet Skis, paddleboarding, and canoeing or kayaking. Tuckahoe has long been the main hub of the township—it is rich in history and has friendly people who are happy to talk about their village.

Middletown's Bailey house, the birthplace of longtime Upper Township resident Jerry Bailey, is shown in this 1910 photograph. Originally built in the early 1800s, it was located on the edge of the meadow near Cedar Run Creek and was moved here in about 1865. Around 1872, it was owned by Daniel Bailey, a boatbuilder at Corson Shipyard at Cedar Swamp Creek. In 1861, he supposedly launched the first three-masted schooner to be built in Cape May County, the *Electa Bailey*. (Courtesy of Grace and Tom Garrity.)

This is a rare postcard of John H. Reed's Triangle service station, located two miles south of Tuckahoe in Middletown. It later became the popular Triton Bar, owned by the Cleak family. The Cleaks sold it to Vince Milita, who kept it as Triton Bar. The gas pumps had been removed by then. It is currently the site of the popular Levari's Seafood & American Grill. (Courtesy of Grace and Tom Garrity.)

Fourth of July parades have long been popular in every small town in America. Here, local Tuckahoe residents proudly ride their horses in a Fourth of July parade around 1900. The photograph was taken in downtown Tuckahoe, just past the intersection of Mill Road and Main Street. (Courtesy of Merry and Joe May.)

Performing at local bandstands and in parades, the Tuckahoe Marching Band was renowned for its music, and residents really enjoyed the band's bass drummer, Mason "Spoodles" Ingersoll. Known for his skilled drumming, he was a popular person in Tuckahoe in the 1920s and 1930s. (Courtesy of Judy Rogers and Carol Foster.)

Before there was a separate post office in Tuckahoe, the post office was located on the first floor of a rooming house (Cushionotto's), shown here, located at 2240 Main Street. The building stands today and still has the room numbers posted on doors. The rooming house was next door to the original Tuckahoe Hotel. Note the 1910-era enclosed coupe parked out front. Today, the post office is at 2250 Route 50. (Courtesy of Merry and Joe May.)

This is a wonderful photograph of kids playing under the tree in front of the Hope Gandy house on Main Street in Tuckahoe. A store was attached to the right of the building. The popular Stille's Garage is seen just north and left of the building. (Courtesy of Merry and Joe May.)

This is a 1910 photograph of the Lilburn Hess house. Hess was the man who started and later built the Tuckahoe National Bank. It is not known when the house was razed, but it became the site of May's Garage, owned by contributor Joe May's father, and is now a vacant lot. (Courtesy of Lynne Dress.)

This is a postcard of the Tuckahoe National Bank on Main Street from around 1910. The bank was robbed in 1925, and the bank president, Edwin Tomlin, was murdered while cashier Edward Rice and his wife were beaten with blackjacks. The gunshot to Tomlin's head ricocheted off the face of the bank's clock, which is currently in possession of the Historical Preservation Society of Upper Township. The building still stands today in downtown Tuckahoe and is currently owned by Sharon Lynne and George Dress. (Courtesy of Barbara Horan.)

This is a great interior shot of the original Tuckahoe Bank, which was built around 1909. The entire facade was made of mahogany, and everyone who saw it was amazed at its beauty. There were two windows (one each for deposits and withdrawals), and behind them, there was a large bank vault, which is still used by the business that occupies the structure today. (Courtesy of Marge and Stoddard Bixby.)

Located across from the bank building on Main Street, the Davis Luncheonette and Kandy Kitchen was a popular spot in downtown Tuckahoe. This photograph from the 1920s shows that the Masonic lodge met upstairs in this building. (Courtesy of Lynne Dress.)

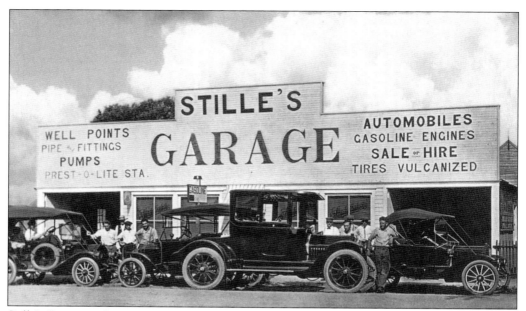

Stille's Garage in downtown Tuckahoe on Main Street across from the post office was a popular auto repair business that also sold engines, well points, pumps, tires, and other equipment. It had a single gas pump and became a full-service Texaco station after 1925. This photograph was probably taken in about 1915 as evidenced by the cars parked out front, which appear to include early Model Ts and a 1913-era enclosed Chevrolet or Cadillac. (Courtesy of Merry and Joe May.)

This is the Hope Gandy house and store on Main Street in downtown Tuckahoe. The small store, attached on the right, later became the Bell Telephone switchboard operators' office. The switchboard handled operator-controlled phone calls until 1961, when dial-tone service was substituted, finally bringing the area into the modern era. (Courtesy of Lynne Dress.)

A Kodak Brownie camera was probably used to take this 1961 photograph of the Bell Telephone switchboard operators on their last night on the job before dial-tone service was fully operational and their services were no longer needed. Grace Butler Garrity is at far left. (Courtesy of Grace and Tom Garrity.)

Tuckahoe's first volunteer fire department was housed here in a converted barn/garage on Main Street in the early 1920s. The Presbyterian church is on the right. (Courtesy of Merry and Joe May.)

The Tuckahoe fire department had a newer building by the 1940s, as evidenced by what appear to be 1940s Nash vehicles. All meetings were held in the upstairs rooms. The current firehouse is located on the same property on Main Street. (Courtesy of Karen Behr.)

The Hagelgans' original grocery and variety store was downtown, where Tuckahoe Bike Shop is located today. Porcelain advertisements on the outside of the building are for Cinco Cigars on the front and for a brand of cheroots on the side. (Cigars were more popular until after World War I, when cigarettes were included in soldiers' rations.) The Hagelgans lived next to their store. Later, the store expanded into a larger building and even a movie house complete with a piano, which was formerly used to play the scores of silent movies. (Courtesy of Merry and Joe May.)

The Hagelgan store expanded and was later purchased around 1948 to become Ann Porter's store, which it remained from the 1950s into the 2000s. It stopped being used as a movie house in the 1930s, and became the one-stop spot for a quick purchase of items not found anywhere else locally. Note the projection booth out in front on the second floor. (Courtesy of Merry and Joe May.)

This beautiful home with the large front porch on the east side of Main Street in Tuckahoe is today the location of the popular Tuckahoe Cheesecake Factory. The photograph was taken in about 1910. Note the buildings that are not there on Main Street anymore! (Courtesy of Barbara Horan.)

Tuckahoe Academy, which housed grades one through four, is shown in this wonderful photograph. The building was constructed around 1861 off Route 50 in downtown Tuckahoe. The school had first and second grades on the first floor and third and fourth grades on the second floor; each floor had its own potbelly stove. Sometime after the new Upper Township Elementary School was built in Marmora, and the villages would no longer have their own schools, this building was razed in the early 1950s. (Courtesy of Barbara Horan.)

Four- and fifth-grade students of Tuckahoe Academy are pictured in 1933. By this time, the school had an additional two-room school built in 1926 and was possibly used for the first through sixth grades. Lilian Beebe was the teacher of these very modern-looking students. (Courtesy of Barbara Horan.)

This is a photograph of the 1919 class of Tuckahoe High School. The brick school building was constructed 11 years prior for about $7,000. Frances Theresa Parker, Larry Sharp's mother, is on the far left of the second row. Future Upper Township teacher Lucy Regine is next to her. Frances lived in Corbin City and traveled every day to come to the high school. The Tuckahoe Academy can be seen just beyond the building on the left side. (Courtesy of Larry Sharp.)

Parked in front of the Tuckahoe High School building is the Upper Township school bus with its driver posing for the camera. The children are seated precariously on benches, facing left and right, in the back of this car-turned-bus. The year is about 1920. The old high school still has all its front windows in place; they would soon be bricked over for an unknown reason. (Courtesy of Barbara Horan.)

Tuckahoe Junior High School's eighth-grade class of 1946 was photographed behind the school for better sunlight. Out front, the spreading trees created too much shade. Grace Butler is in the second row, third from left. (Courtesy of Grace and Tom Garrity.)

This is a 1940s photograph of the Tuckahoe Middle School, fifth and sixth grades, built in 1926. The building's two front windows have by now been enclosed. The building was used until the opening of the new elementary school in Marmora, and it later became a school for the Seventh-Day Adventist church in Marmora. (Courtesy of the Cape May County Historical and Genealogical Museum.)

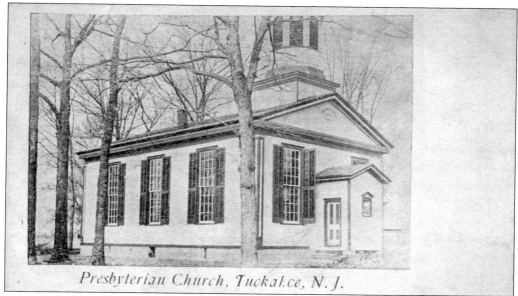

Presbyterian Church, Tuckahoe, N. J.

Shown here in 1906, Tuckahoe Presbyterian Church lives on, and the building remains standing as the home of the Daughters of America. The structure, which was built in the 1850s, housed a Presbyterian church for some time before being laid down, probably in the 1930s; it then became the home of the Pomona Grange before the Daughters of America in 1964. The building is currently owned by the Tuckahoe Volunteer Fire Department. (Courtesy of Corville Griner.)

This photograph of the Daughters of America was taken in their meeting place above the firehouse before moving to the upstairs of the A&P building and then buying the empty Presbyterian Church in 1964. The Daughters of America, Tuckahoe Council No. 49 of the National Daughters of America has a long and storied history in the community. (Courtesy of Gail Wriggins.)

This beautiful pastoral photograph shows tree-lined downtown Tuckahoe. A local horse-drawn jitney is being followed by a dog as it makes its way north on Main Street toward the bridge to Corbin City or west toward Marshallville on what was then Route 47. The jitney has just passed Mill Road (later Reading Avenue). (Courtesy of Barbara Horan.)

This photograph, taken in about 1912, is of the old gristmill across from Mill Creek. The mill was in operation in the 1850s and 1860s. The two people pictured are Jean Haines Anderson and her daughter Margaret, who later married the Reverend Folger, a Methodist minister in Tuckahoe in about 1930. Margaret later became the mother of Harry P. Folger III and Jean Folger Campbell. (Courtesy of Corville Griner.)

Tuckahoe Junction was built in 1894 and served the Pennsylvania & Reading Railroad. It brought notoriety to this small Cape May County village, and the area around the station became a rail hub for repairs and the transport of goods out of the area to markets far away. This photograph was taken in about 1910. (Courtesy of Barbara Horan.)

Engine No. 12 is loaded with coal, powered by steam, and pulling its tender and two passenger cars. It is manned by an engineer, fireman, conductor, and crew, in this early-20th-century photograph, taken at a stop in Tuckahoe while probably on its way to the shore. (Courtesy of Merry and Joe May.)

Here is the Tuckahoe train station pump house with its proud three-man crew; the photograph was taken in 1910. (Courtesy of Merry and Joe May.)

This is a beautiful 1940s photograph of peaceful Reading Avenue (formerly Mill Road), taken looking east toward the station and downtown Tuckahoe. Dare Robinson, Corville Griner's uncle, built his lovely home here himself after serving in the Navy at Pearl Harbor both during and after the attack by Japan on December 7, 1941. (Courtesy of Corville Griner.)

It was a busy day in 1900, as evidenced by the piles of full tomato baskets at Cleaver's Diamont canning factory, located across from the Tuckahoe Train Station. The cannery predominantly canned tomatoes, but also canned other vegetables brought to the cannery by local farmers or by train. (Courtesy of Karen Behr.)

The Diamont canning factory was later sold and became a source of production for other interesting items. Dr. Alison Howe Price worked here for a while and is credited with inventing the medicine Maalox. Later, the building was sold to the DeSantis family, who made it a feed store. It closed in the 1980s and was later used by the township for public functions. It has since been bought and taken over by a catering and antique business known as the Everly. (Courtesy of Merry and Joe May.)

"Picturesque Tuckahoe" is advertised in the *Philadelphia Inquirer* to lure customers to come and buy parcels of land and have a place at the shore in New Jersey. Lots were advertised for a dollar down with the rest financed through the company. Although elaborate maps of the lots were drawn, this development did not succeed. (Courtesy of Barbara Horan.)

The A&P grocery store was popular in downtown Tuckahoe and was located across from Stille's Garage. In this early 1930s photograph, locals Francis Powell (left) and Al Hand are seated out front of the store. Al was the manager of the store, which burned down in the 1932 fire that destroyed the Tuckahoe Hotel and its garage next door. According to a sign in the window, four boxes of spaghetti sold for 25¢. (Courtesy of Karen Behr.)

This great late 1930s photograph of downtown Tuckahoe was taken several years after the major fire that took out three buildings on the west side of Main Street a few years earlier. Along the left are the post office, the empty lots where the hotel, its garage, and the A&P grocery store used to be, and the Grange building. On the right are the Hess house, the Tuckahoe Bank, the Hope Gandy house/Bell Telephone office, and Stille's Texaco station. (Courtesy of Barbara Horan.)

This photograph of the old Tuckahoe Hotel was taken around 1910. It was owned by the Johnny and Kris Kirchoff family. Not too long after this, the hotel burned to the ground; another fire destroyed the second building in 1932. (Courtesy of Lynne Dress.)

The second Tuckahoe Hotel, built after the first fire and shown here in the late 1920s, was renowned for its restaurant; the food was prepared in the kitchen by cook–hotel manager Mrs. Chattin, seen here at the front door with a patron. Sadly, this building burned down in 1932. Newspaper accounts claim the fire started in the kitchen and took with it the garage and the A&P grocery store. (Courtesy of Lynne Dress.)

Built in 1940, Robinette's Diner, popular in the 1960s and 1970s, was a Silk City Diner model, manufactured by the Paterson Vehicle Company. This photograph of the diner shows it as it exists today. Robinette's Diner was bought and refurbished in 1990 by Tim De Filippis. It was eventually sold and is now called the Tuckahoe Family Diner. It has expanded and includes outdoor dining now. (Photograph by the author.)

This previously unpublished photograph is of the intersection of Main Street (left) and Mount Pleasant Avenue, known by locals as the "Flat Iron." Little is known about the building on the corner, but it is thought to have been a small hotel/rooming house. Benjamin Marshall's dry goods store is down Mount Pleasant Avenue on the right past the corner. (Courtesy of Corville Griner.)

This is a bright and crisp photograph of the new Masonic lodge, built right on the Flat Iron corner in downtown Tuckahoe where Main Street and Mount Pleasant Avenue intersect. The lodge was previously located upstairs in the A&P building. This photograph was likely taken soon after the building's completion in the early 1930s. (Courtesy of Corville Griner.)

In this rare interior photograph, Benjamin Marshall stands behind the counter in his dry goods store across from and down the street from the Flat Iron corner in downtown Tuckahoe. (Courtesy of Lynne Dress.)

This photograph of the original Tuckahoe Methodist Episcopal Church, built in 1829, was taken in the 1920s or early 1930s. The church burned to the ground on Christmas Eve 1939 due to a chimney fire that had been smoldering all night, unknown by those at the service. The fire department had hoses stretching all the way to the river to bring water to help put out the blaze, which could be seen for miles around. (Courtesy of Merry and Joe May.)

This photograph shows the remains of the Tuckahoe Methodist Church after it tragically burned down on Christmas Eve 1939. The building has been completely gutted. The photograph is labeled December 24, but it was most likely taken on Christmas Day. After the Christmas Eve service, the church was locked, and everyone went home. The blaze was seen as far away as Woodbine. (Courtesy of Merry and Joe May.)

This photograph of the newly rebuilt Tuckahoe Methodist Church was taken around 1940. The church reopened in 1941. It took just about one year to completely rebuild the church. This church has its first of three steeples that were rebuilt throughout the succeeding decades. (Courtesy of Lynne Dress.)

The Upper Township Red Cross nursing class of 1943 poses for a photograph inside the sanctuary of Tuckahoe Methodist Church. These women were taught nursing skills, first aid and bandage preparation, and other skills as part of the home front war effort while full-time nurses were aiding the military overseas. (Courtesy of Grace and Tom Garrity.)

This is a 1908 photograph of the Methodist church's parsonage when Tuckahoe Methodist Church had a full-time pastor. The home is on the left side of Main Street, just past the intersection of Routes 50 and 49. (Courtesy of Barbara Horan.)

The Wittkamp American Legion post is on the lot next to the west corner of Routes 49 and 50, facing Main Street; previously, the group met upstairs in the Grange building. The building, at 2286 Route 50, later became a private residence, and then Hometown Lumber, owned by the DeSantis family, in the 1990s. (Courtesy of Corville Griner.)

Shown here in the 1940s is the original building of the Langley funeral home. The sign by the front door reads, "John L. Langley, Funeral Director." This building was quite possibly originally a tavern, built in the late 18th century. It was bought by John Langley's father, Samuel G. Langley, in 1905 as a funeral director's home and business. The business is now owned by Paul Loveland III, the current funeral director. (Courtesy of Paul Loveland III.)

This photograph of the Tuckahoe River Bridge was taken in about 1905 when the bridge was a swing-type bridge (unusual for the area), which allowed ship traffic to pass along the river. The bridge tender's house can be seen at left. (Courtesy of Barbara Horan.)

This view from the Tuckahoe River Bridge shows the boatbuilding and boat service businesses along the Tuckahoe (Williamsburg) side of the river. This area still bustles today with boatbuilding and repairs, done principally by Yank Boat Works. (Courtesy of Larry Sharp.)

The new state highway bridge across the Tuckahoe River is shown here in 1926. The drawbridge was state of the art at the time, and crossed the river from then Williamsburg (South Tuckahoe) to North Tuckahoe (Corbin City). (Courtesy of Lynne Dress.)

This is a fascinating shot of Dr. Randolph Marshall Jr. mixing a medication at his counter, while brother Dr. Joseph Marshall sits in a chair reading a newspaper. This building still stands today in downtown Tuckahoe as an antiques shop. An exterior photograph of the building is on page 107. (Courtesy of Karen Behr.)

Although not directly in the city limits, the Aetna iron furnace and foundry is listed as being located in Tuckahoe as early as 1898. The furnace was built in 1816, and by the 20th century, it was completely gone from view. (Courtesy of Lynne Dress.)

Here is a very fine school photograph taken in 1910 of the North Tuckahoe School, later the Corbin City School, with Rodney van Gilder as the teacher. The town across the Tuckahoe River, formerly North Tuckahoe, was renamed Corbin City in the 1930s by the state legislature and was thereafter officially part of Atlantic County. (Courtesy of Paul Loveland III.)

Eight

MARSHALLVILLE

There are no official signs directing travelers to Marshallville. Traveling south down Route 49 from Millville or Port Elizabeth (once Route 47), a left turn at the intersection of Route 557, Woodbine Road, leads there.

Marshallville was once a bustling town with few homes but several thriving businesses. Glassmaking was the primary industry, but boatbuilding was also present. There was a store, a tavern, a school (which also served as the meetinghouse), docks, and factories. Margaret Folger wrote that Marshallville was once "a busy thoroughfare with ocean going sailboats traveling up and down its waters. There was also much business in operation on both sides of the river."

Marshallville not only produced glass but also leather, wood, cranberries, and farm produce. Boats could travel as far as Head of the River, outside of Marshallville in Cumberland County, where the Aetna iron furnace and foundry produced a variety of iron goods, even cannonballs for the War of 1812.

In the earliest days, both sides of the river were called Tuckahoe, but in 1922, the Atlantic County side (North Tuckahoe) became known as Corbin City, while South Tuckahoe (Williamsburg) remained simply Tuckahoe. Randall Marshall, a prominent Port Elizabeth businessman, bought forest land below Head of the River. He and his son-in-law Frederick Stanger bought 5,000 acres in 1811, which included a mill along Mill Creek that flows into the Tuckahoe River. This land was partly in Cumberland County and partly in Cape May County.

Folger states that "Randall owned one quarter of the Union Glass Company along with a tannery and store in Port Elizabeth, but Union Glass works was closing and since Stanger was a glass blower, the two men decided to move one glass furnace to the banks of the river in 1814, purchasing 450 acres adjoining the first tract. The business flourished and grew to a four-furnace company, and so was created the town of Marshallville."

Marshallville was founded for one purpose, long forgotten: manufacturing window glass and bottles. There was clearly a great desire for these types of glass both with the growth of buildings and the growth of patent medicines and bottled drinks. Union Glass Works was dissolved in Port Elizabeth, but for a time, Randal Marshall kept his home there and came to work on horseback every day. An original furnace from Port Elizabeth was brought over to Marshallville and Marshall pioneered the making of window glass. He built about 20 homes for the workers and larger ones for his family members. Two workers' families who still have descendants in South Jersey are the Hanns and the Wheatons.

There once was a schoolhouse that doubled as a Quaker meetinghouse on Sundays, a small Methodist chapel (Head of the River Church up the road was still the principal local church), a tavern, a limekiln, a shipyard, and a country store that also housed the post office.

One narrow road led from Head of the River to Williamsburg, as Tuckahoe was called then, the southern section of what is now Tuckahoe. The branch through the village became known as Marshallville Road.

There is an old brick house built by John Stille, and to the right of it was a home built in 1840 by William Burley. In 1847, Burley built the house for Mary Marshall, later to be used by the glass company. There were once lime kilns along the road used for calcium carbonate production to produce quicklime used in the making of both mortar and glass. On the right was a lovely home built for Randal Marshall's daughter Mary, who married Ebenezer Seeley. A tavern was also built nearby, but both of these structures were razed.

The local company store, which housed the post office, was the heart and soul of the village. The store is gone, and in 1930 a house was erected on the site. Scrip was issued by the glass factory to be used at the company store.

Shipping and boating were the main form of transportation, but there was another road that led to Dennisville. On one corner of this road, Randall Marshall had a house built in 1818 for his oldest son, Thomas Chew Marshall, who was also a glass gaffer (blower). He and his wife, Experience, raised 14 children. Two of their children learned to cut glass in the factory. Randolph, the youngest son of Randal and Mary, attended the School of Pharmacy in Philadelphia and started his practice in Marshallville. Later, he established a shop in Tuckahoe in partnership with his brother, who had become a physician and practiced in the area.

Thomas Chew Marshall built another brick house for himself at age 70 to be near his glassworks and his children. He died in 1841 before he could move from Port Elizabeth and never lived in the home. He was buried in the Quaker cemetery. The Thomas Chew Marshall house still stands today, occupied by descendant Harry P. Folger III, although shingles cover the original cedar clapboards. It has its original windows and glass on the back. Randal Marshall built another large house near Thomas and Experience Marshall's home. Most of the homes there had been constructed from local trees, but three brick houses were built later.

In the early 1800s, there was no bridge across the creek until a covered bridge was built in 1841. This bridge lasted into the 20th century. The next bridge, built in 1901, has since been destroyed and was not replaced, cutting Marshallville in two.

A brick house was built in 1835 by Randall Marshall for his youngest child, Randolph, who later became a doctor. He and his wife, Sarah Hughes, raised several children, two of whom also became doctors. His other son, Dr. Joseph Marshall, a physician and brother of Dr. Randolph Marshall, a pharmacist, were in business together in the area for many years. The Marshall brothers' pharmacy building/doctor's office was built in 1877 and still stands today in downtown Tuckahoe as an antiques store.

Marshallville is a treasure to the township both for its rich history and the beauty of its old homes along Mill Creek and the Tuckahoe River.

Although the joint doctor's office and pharmacy of Drs. Joseph Marshall and Randolph Marshall Jr. was located in Tuckahoe, the building's connection to Marshallville has always been clear. Specializing in children's diseases, Randolph Marshall Jr. graduated from Jefferson Medical College in 1877, and in the same year, Marshall Jr. and his brother Joseph Corson Marshall constructed a building on Main Street in Tuckahoe. It served as both a medical office and pharmacy until 1890. (Courtesy of Joan Berkey.)

The Andrew J. Steelman house is located on Marshallville Road. Steelman was a glass blower and supervisor at Marshallville Glassworks. He owned land just down the road from Dr. Randolph Marshall Sr.'s house, next to the school property along the Tuckahoe River. (Courtesy of HPSUT.)

The John and Anne Stille house still stands today in Marshallville. The brick house was built in 1836 in the Federal style and is almost identical to the Dr. Randolph Marshall Sr. house. John was a partner in the Marshall-Stille Company, which ran the general store. On the 1850 census, he is listed as a farmer. Garet Garrett, financial writer for major New York newspapers, owned the house from 1925 until his death in 1954. The property under his ownership was called Yellow Hill Farm. (Courtesy of Joan Berkey.)

The Dr. Randolph Marshall Sr. house was built in 1834 by his father, Randall Marshall, the founder of Union Glass works in Marshallville. Dr. Marshall graduated from medical school at the University of Pennsylvania the year the house was built. Architectural historian Joan Berkey stated, "His laxity in imposing and collecting fees and his generosity to the general public alone prevented his accumulation of great wealth." (Courtesy of Joan Berkey.)

The Marshallville covered bridge was first built in 1841 and lasted into the 20th century. Due to structural issues, it was replaced with an open bridge, which has since become derelict and unusable. This photograph was probably taken around the turn of the 20th century. (Courtesy of Jean Campbell and Harry P. Folger III.)

Randall Marshall and his wife, Mary, built this house between 1820 and 1840 but never resided in it as a couple. Instead, they lived in Port Elizabeth, and Marshall traveled on horseback every day to Marshallville for work. Randall died in 1841. Mary and her unmarried daughter moved in. Structural evidence indicates that the building was later altered to have a porch on the south and east sides, but the porch was removed some time ago. The home is currently owned by Edward Bixby Jr. (Courtesy of Joan Berkey.)

Margaret Anderson Folger, Harry P. Folger III's mother, is pictured with her uncle Edgar Sheppard. The Marshallville company store is visible in the background. This store, where workers usually paid for their purchases with scrip, was built for the Marshallville glass factory along the Tuckahoe River. (Courtesy of Jean Campbell and Harry P. Folger III.)

This is a rare photograph of the Marshallville School, shown in the distance at right in the early 20th century along the dirt Marshallville Road leading to Woodbine Road. The school was beside the property of Dr. Randolph Marshall Sr.'s home and was frequently used as a Sunday meetinghouse for worship services. The school was moved to Cold Spring Village many years ago and restored. It can still be seen today. (Courtesy of Jean Campbell and Harry P. Folger III.)

The Thomas Chew Marshall house still stands today on the corner of Marshallville and Woodbine Roads. (On the northern corner opposite once stood the Steelman Tavern, which dated to the 18th century.) The Thomas Chew Marshall house was built in 1818 and has been continuously inhabited ever since by the ancestors of Margaret Folger and her son, Harry P. Folger III. (Courtesy of Jean Folger Campbell and Harry P. Folger III.)

The Marshallville School was set up for the glass factory workers' children. (Note its distinctive eyebrow window above the door.) Located on Marshallville Road, it was situated along the river, next to the Steelman property. It was later moved to Cold Spring Village, where it was lovingly and carefully restored. (Courtesy of Jean Campbell and Harry P. Folger III.)

This photograph taken in the early 1900s and labeled Marshallville Avenue looking east. It shows the future Route 47 and eventually Route 49; the road to Tuckahoe from Port Elizabeth and Millville. This photograph clearly shows farm buildings that still stand and the Tuckahoe Methodist Episcopal Church in the distance. (Courtesy of Barbara Horan.)

Head of the River Church, a meetinghouse located up Route 49 from Marshallville at the head of the Tuckahoe River, is included in this chapter because of the importance of the church to local Methodists. In this turn-of-the-century photograph, an iron fence has been added around the graveyard. It was removed during World War II and melted down for the war effort. (Courtesy of Grace and Tom Garrity.)

Nine

STEELMANTOWN

Steelmantown, once an area filled with cranberry bogs, acres of farms, and pitch pine forests, is now a small village leading out of Marshallville on the way to Woodbine along Woodbine Road from the intersection at Route 49.

Harry P. Folger III wrote in the 1989 *A History of Upper Township and Its Villages* that "It was a busy place at one time consisting of homes, farms, cranberry bogs, a cranberry processing house, a school, a church, with a graveyard, and two mills. One of the mills was located on Mill Creek near the present Woodbine Road and is known today as Great-g Mill." It is not known when the name of Steelmantown was first used, but it surely relates to residents in the area named Steelman. Much of the land in the area was owned by Hezekiah Steelman.

Steelmantown is the westernmost village of the township between Tuckahoe and Woodbine on the direct route of Woodbine Road–Washington Avenue (Route 557). It is heavily wooded, and roads branch off in many directions. It is surrounded by Belleplain State Forest and the Cape May National Wildlife Refuge.

Steelmantown once had two mills, and one of them was Richard Steelman's sawmill. The cranberry bogs are now gone—dried up and covered with plant growth. At one time, cranberry production was a vibrant aspect of the local economy. Years ago, this area with its abundant pitch pine trees was also a center for the production of tar and pitch used for shipbuilding on the Tuckahoe River. Three-masted schooners, like the *Adella Corson*, were built on the river no doubt using materials produced in Steelmantown. The kilns, once so numerous, are all gone with no evidence of their existence.

Edward Bixby Jr., whose ancestors once resided throughout Steelmantown, still remembers the buildings that dotted Steelmantown Road, Narrows Road, and Woodbine Road. One structure was an icehouse that was constructed with inner concrete walls to help insulate ice cut from millponds and prevent it from melting. Bixby now owns and operates the Steelmantown Cemetery on Steelmantown Road where the school and old chapel (which burned down in 1910) once stood. A certified natural burial ground, which requires that there be no embalming, crypts, nor caskets, it is the only green cemetery on the East Coast. The old cemetery itself has been restored and cared for, off and on, over the years. An Eagle Scout project by local resident Brian Horan involved the placement of 135 brick markers upon the unmarked graves of former residents of the Woodbine Developmental Center. They had been buried between 1958 and 1979 by Langley Funeral Home owner Jack Langley, who also owned the cemetery at the time. A Woodbine Developmental Center resident said, "The lost boys of Woodbine had been found."

Driving on Woodbine Road toward Woodbine, the road forks to yet another small village—Martintown. Little is known of this old village, but it has an exclusively African American cemetery and an African Evangelist church founded by Pastor Ruby Macky of Woodbine. Steelmantown had a large number of African Americans who lived back on Homestead Avenue, plying trades such as ragman, tinker, knife sharpener, firewood supplier, and produce seller, to name but a few.

The area of Steelmantown closest to Martintown/Woodbine was once known as Woodbine Heights and was owned by Woodbine, which sold the area to Upper Township in 1908. There was also a charcoal business in the area, made possible by all of the trees.

There were terrible fires in the area dating to 1880. This first forest fire was huge and burned thousands of acres not far from Steelmantown. The fire began at Jones Mill near Manumuskin's Pennsylvania Railroad station and burned from there all the way to below the Belleplain Station along Port Road and Belleplain Road to Steelmantown. It must have been a devastating fire with no ability of local municipalities to put it out.

A number of Steelmantown residents are buried in the 1791 Head of the River Methodist Church Cemetery as well as the Steelmantown Cemetery. Head of the River is west of Marshallville. It is near the point where Atlantic County, Cumberland County, and Cape May County join together and is known as the place where navigation on the Tuckahoe River ceases.

It is hard to imagine the industries that went on here. Though the Benezett Mill, the cranberry bogs, and the shipbuilding all once thrived here, little evidence remains. The farms and orchards have given way to comfortable homes. Plans for development on a wider scale in Steelmantown were blocked by the Pinelands Act; however, individual builders created little developments of homes along Woodbine Road. There are roads perpendicular to it, like Narrows Road and Steelmantown Road, leading back to Homestead Road. A scant few older structures remain in Steelmantown and serve as a reminder of the different way of life that existed here.

Robert Frost wrote, "Good fences make good neighbors." If that is so, then the neighbors of Steelmantown, many of whom are not exactly close by, look out for one another and try to be good neighbors.

This is one of the older homes in Steelmantown; it was constructed on the marshy ground between Marshallville and Woodbine along Woodbine Road. It was thought to be occupied by the Layton family and had no running water nor electricity until the 1950s. This building was gone by the 1990s. The photograph is attributed to lifelong Tuckahoe resident and avid historian Raymond Young. (Courtesy of HPSUT.)

This photograph from the 1930s shows a home on Steelmantown Road that once was transformed into an icehouse, as evidenced by the concrete walls used for insulation. The first owner of the icehouse who transformed it back to a residence was the Champion family. The home was later purchased by the Barber family. (Courtesy of Edward Bixby Jr.)

This 1930s photograph shows two young mule riders, Sam (left) and Arthur Barber, by the barn on the new Barber homestead, which was recently purchased from the Champion family. (Courtesy of Edward Bixby Jr.)

This 1960s photograph, taken by local historian Raymond Young, shows the once-abandoned Steelmantown Cemetery. The cemetery contains graves of many local residents as well as men who died in the Revolutionary and Civil Wars. (Courtesy of HPSUT.)

The original Steelmantown Chapel once sat on the grounds of the current cemetery. It was built in 1910 by Samuel Barber and later burned down. Near where this original chapel once stood was the Steelmantown School, which burned down during the Great Steelmantown Fire of the 1890s. The fire destroyed hundreds of acres in the village, and the school was never rebuilt. A smaller replica of the chapel was built by the Edward Bixby Sr. family, the current owners of the Steelmantown Cemetery. (Courtesy of Barbara Horan.)

This is a 1960 photograph by local historian Raymond Young of the grave of local Civil War soldier Hezekiah Creamer, son of Jacob and Rebecca Creamer. Born on January 23, 1831, he died on July 9, 1864, serving in a New Jersey regiment of the Union Army and could have been killed in battle leading up to the Confederate attacks on Washington, DC, by Confederate general Jubal Early. (Courtesy of HPSUT.)

This is a 1960 photograph of the rebuilt Steelmantown Cemetery Chapel. It still stands in the Steelmantown Cemetery. (Courtesy of Barbara Horan.)

Pictured in this sad Raymond Young photograph is the grave of infant Norma J. Layton, who was born on September 22 and died less than two months later on November 1. Layton family members were numerous in the village of Steelmantown. Young children were especially vulnerable to disease and frequently died young, which was why so many families had large numbers of children. (Courtesy of HPSUT.)

Ten

STRATHMERE

The Lenni Lenape were here first, coming in the summer to the beaches to fish and gather clams and oysters. In addition to the Corsons who came later, there were the Garretsons, Mackeys, and Van Gilders. With the land gradually being discovered by fishermen, there needed to be a better way to reach the island. Fortunately, railroads were being built throughout South Jersey by the late 19th century.

In 1881, the West Jersey Railroad, which ran from Sea Isle to Cape May, built the Sea Isle Junction. By 1884, the railroad extended to Ocean City. The train brought visitors from Philadelphia, Camden, and northwest Jersey, so the area became a serious tourist destination. The West Jersey Railroad began to decline, and a merger with the Reading Railroad resulted in bankruptcy. Eventually, the Townsend's Inlet and Stone Harbor connections were dismantled. This downturn in train travel was no doubt caused by the advent of the automobile and its meteoric rise in popularity.

Strathmere is the only island village of Upper Township. It can only be reached by boat or bridge. The bridges extend from the south from Avalon and then along the main road through Sea Isle City or directly from Ocean City in the north. It is bordered on one side by the ocean, and edging the other side are soft, quiet meadows and winding creeks, with occasional ibis, gull, or duck rising from its shores and gullies.

John and Peter Corson were among the first to brave this territory and establish homes. The land on the south side of the inlet became known simply as Corson's Inlet, which was later changed to Strathmere in about 1909–1912. The area of Strathmere is only 1.5 miles long and 2 blocks wide. The whole of Ludlam's Island, which is shared between Sea Isle City and Strathmere, was once entirely owned by Sea Isle City. A couple named John and Jenny Burk once owned all of Ludlam's Island. In 1881, the land was deeded to Matilda Landis and her attorney Charles K. Landis, founder of both Vineland and Hammonton, New Jersey, who created the Sea Isle Improvement Corporation to develop this property. The Corson's Inlet end of the island was sold by the City of Sea Isle to Upper Township in 1905 for $31,500 ($817,000 today) to pay the city's bills. This was a bargain for this piece of oceanfront land.

The island was quiet in the winter, but come summer, Strathmere came to life with day-trippers, weekly renters, and fishermen from Philadelphia and other New Jersey communities.

Downtown Strathmere has its own post office, a church, firehouse, and several restaurants. In the early 20th century, there were two large hotels that had railroad lines coming close to them to allow travelers to disembark.

Over the years, as development increased at an enthusiastic level, developers sold parcels of land to those desiring island or beachfront properties. Venturing south along Commonwealth Avenue, the homes spread out, and several are built right on the beach.

Many residents and visitors are enthusiastic to save and take care of the turtles that cross the road in their quest to get to the dunes and bury their eggs. Their journey is an arduous one, and hundreds are saved every summer by the vigilant populace.

Strathmere had its own school at one time, the Corson's Inlet School, housed in a bungalow owned by John L. Schmidt around 1910. The school had only about 12 to 15 students, ranging from first to eighth grade. The post office was the center of activity since mail was not delivered and had to be picked up daily. The first two hotels in Corson's Inlet were the Wittkamp Hotel and the Whelen Hotel, now the Deauville Inn. The Whelen lodged men who worked on the Pennsylvania Railroad.

One famous bar down the street along the bay was once known as "Dirty Gertie's" (present-day Twisties). Some of the local watering holes, like Dirty Gertie's, were speakeasies during Prohibition, but after it was repealed, they became popular bars.

Roads into Ludlam's island in the beginning were just dirt wagon roads, but a resolution was passed opening a road from the north end to the southeast end of Upper Township and connecting with a road in Sea Isle City. The first bridge was built in the early 20th century, and it eventually became a drawbridge. In 1969, a larger toll bridge was built to replace the old one.

Lifesaving stations were established along the Jersey coast because of the huge growth in ship traffic. These "houses of refuge" manned by the US Lifesaving Service (eventually the Coast Guard) saved hundreds of lives along the coast. It is reported that, from 1806 to 1885, a total of 65 vessels wrecked between Corson's Inlet and Townsend's Inlet alone. In 1878, seven schooners and one steamship were lost. This lifesaving station in Strathmere, moved from the south end of Ocean City in the mid-1920s, was integral in the saving of ships' crews battered by storms and surf. The keeper and his crew, called surfmen, were ever ready to go out in all conditions to save those in peril. During World War I and World War II, many ships were sunk just miles offshore by German U-boats that plied the coastal areas to sink Allied cargo ships.

Whale Beach off Commonwealth Avenue in Strathmere once had a boardwalk, built in about 1911, but this was before the sale of the north end of Ludlam Beach (Corson's Inlet) to Upper Township.

Strathmere continues to support a large crowd of fishers, hunters, surfers, and boaters. Upper Township has been providing lifeguard protection for many of the beaches. The bay side has many docks and businesses to support the boaters who come to the area.

Over the years, hurricanes and nor'easters have been a serious factor in the history of Strathmere and, on occasion, have very nearly spelled its doom. A severe hurricane in 1944 devastated towns of the Jersey Shore, and in 1962, a huge nor'easter crippled the area. The people of Strathmere are extremely resilient, and despite occasional weather adversity, the village remains a vital part of Upper Township.

This aerial photograph, probably taken in the 1920s or 1930s, shows the entrance to Strathmere from Ocean City via Corson's Inlet. The bulkhead and letters are long gone, but this area of Strathmere can still be seen from the bridge. (Courtesy of Strathmere.net.)

This photograph of the Pennsylvania–Reading Seashore Line train is moving frighteningly close between early houses along the tracks leading into Strathmere. Note the long line of passenger cars being pulled behind. This is a full train of tourists. A trainman is walking precariously along a gangplank on the locomotive's engine house. The photograph was taken after 1909–1912, when the name Corson's Inlet was changed to Strathmere. (Courtesy of Strathmere.net.)

The Corson's Inlet train station saw many tourists come to Strathmere for all kinds of recreation. This early photograph was likely taken after a recent storm, as damage to the station is evident. Note the broken windows and missing exterior clapboards. The man at center is Augustus Lutz, a Civil War veteran who worked and lived at the West Jersey Cottage. The man on the right is Gus Wittkamp, the owner of the West Jersey Cottage and the train station manager. (Courtesy of Strathmere.net.)

Strathmere grew in large part because of the railroads that brought thousands of tourists every year to the island. Here are the trainmen for locomotive No. 6070 of the West Jersey Line, which once ran along Commonwealth Avenue, the main thoroughfare of Strathmere. Note the houses close to the tracks at right. (Courtesy of Strathmere.net.)

West Jersey Cottage and Annex, Gus Wittkamp, Corson's Inlet, N. J.

As this photograph's title indicates, the West Jersey Cottage and Annex was built in 1896 and was owned by Gus Wittkamp. It was a very popular destination for tourists, bathers, and fishermen who came to Corson's Inlet (later Strathmere) for leisure. They arrived by trains that took them directly to the resorts. The cottage got its name from the West Jersey Railroad, and the station was directly across from the cottage. (Courtesy of Strathmere.net.)

Fishing at Corson's Inlet, Cape May Co., N. J.

Located at Corson's Inlet, the Whelen Hotel (today's Deauville Inn) was first built and owned by James P. Carothers, who came to America from Ireland in 1862. The original building catered to 100 guests. The Reading Line ran right by the Whelen Hotel on the other side of the dunes at rear and made six stops every day. (Courtesy of Strathmere.net.)

This 1909 postcard portrays visiting New York City fishermen staying at Wittkamp's West Jersey Cottage. They obviously had a successful day of fishing and are proudly showing off their catches; some of them dressed up in fine shirts and ties. (Courtesy of Strathmere.net.)

The Coast Guard building, Lifesaving Station No. 32, in Corson's Inlet was first erected on the Ocean City side of the inlet at Fifty-eighth Street in 1872. Seen here in 1899, the station was enlarged after the devastating storm of 1924, which destroyed the bulkheads in front. In order to save it, the station was moved to the south side of Corson's Inlet and was renamed the Corson's Inlet Coast Guard Station No. 128. Standing in front are the proud crew of the station. (Courtesy of Strathmere.net.)

This is an advertisement from *Strathmere by the Sea*, a promotional booklet. (Corson's Inlet had changed its name to Strathmere sometime between 1909 and 1912.) It was distributed by the Strathmere Corporation, which was trying to develop Strathmere as a resort around 1922. The brochure portrayed happy bathers in the surf, inexpensive fares to the village, and bargain rates on building lots. A complete copy of this interesting booklet is available in the Schiavo-Strathmere Library. (Courtesy of Strathmere.net.)

The Yellow Kid Train, seen in this c. 1900 photograph, was a popular line powered by an engine of the same name. *The Yellow Kid* was a very popular comic strip that ran from 1895 to 1898, first in Pulitzer's *New York World* and then Hearst's New York City newspapers. Ahead of its time, the comic strip was published in a color Sunday supplement with its humor aimed at class and racial issues. It featured the Yellow Kid and other children from the "wrong side of the tracks." (Courtesy of Strathmere.net.)

IN THE HEART OF AMERICA'S PLAYGROUND

STRATHMERE
"BY-THE-SEA"

Philadelphia 60 Miles   Atlantic City 8 Miles
Ocean City (Across the Inlet)

Excellent Train Service $1.50 Daily Excursions

UNEXCELLED BATHING—FISHING SAILING—CRABING

Ocean and Bay Front Lots **$150.00** and up { TERMS TO SUIT

In this c. 1912 photograph, the Strathmere Electric Trolley has just dropped off passengers at Strathmere (note the sign above the awning). Day-trippers seemingly had to exit and enter the roadway by stepping over the train tracks. The dress of the people indicates that it is a warm summer day—perfect weather for a visit. (Courtesy of Strathmere.net.)

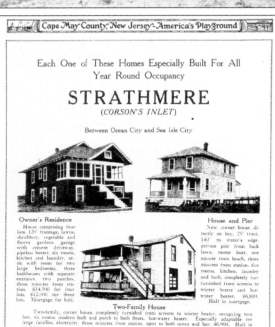

This page from a c. 1912–1915 promotional brochure shows how homes, built by real estate developer E.M. Fenton, looked in those days. Advertisements in newspapers touted Cape May County, and specifically Corson's Inlet/Strathmere, New Jersey, as America's playground. Pictured here are just a few of the sample cottages that could be built to suit the buyer's specifications. (Courtesy of Strathmere.net.)

BIBLIOGRAPHY

Beitel, Herb, and Nancy Enc. *Cape May County*. Virginia Beach, VA: Donning Co. Publishers, 1988.

Berkey, Joan. *Early Architecture of Cape May County*. Cape May Court House, NJ: Cape May County Historical & Genealogical Society, 2008.

————. *A Survey of 80 Historic Buildings and Sites in Upper Township, Cape May County NJ*. Cape May County & Heritage Commission, 2017.

Boyer, George F., and Jane P. Cunningham. *Cape May County Story*. Egg Harbor City, NJ: Laureate Press, 1975.

Craig, Stanley. *History of Petersburg*. Tuckahoe, NJ: Herald Press, 1913.

Dorwart, Jeffrey. *Cape May County, NJ*. New Brunswick, NJ: Rutgers University Press, 1996.

Folger, Margaret. "Marshallville." *A History of Upper Township and Its Villages*. Marmora, NJ: Historical Preservation Society of Upper Township, 1989.

Robinson, Edwin B. "Tuckahoe Remembered: A Personal Recollection of the Early 1900s." unpublished manuscript, 1982.

Speck, Florence. "Early History of Upper Precinct." *A History of Upper Township and Its Villages*. Marmora, NJ: Historical Preservation Society of Upper Township, 1989.

DISCOVER THOUSANDS OF LOCAL HISTORY BOOKS FEATURING MILLIONS OF VINTAGE IMAGES

Arcadia Publishing, the leading local history publisher in the United States, is committed to making history accessible and meaningful through publishing books that celebrate and preserve the heritage of America's people and places.

Find more books like this at
www.arcadiapublishing.com

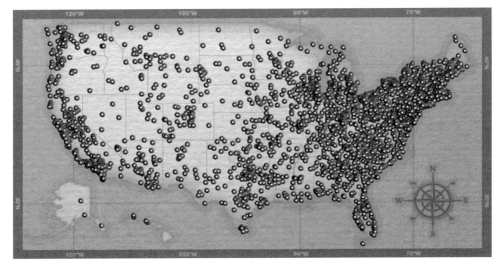

Search for your hometown history, your old stomping grounds, and even your favorite sports team.